SELF WILL

Roy L. Wyble, III

From the Author

This book is written in dedication to my daughter and her generation. Although current health and science proves no cure exists for people in an active state of addiction, there is a long term cure. We are that cure. We must work together to create a culture in which our children have every opportunity to succeed in life. For some, this involves the education necessary in making decisions to abstain from drugs and alcohol. Prevention is key to the people with similar genetics to mine. Your children will not have a problem as long as the chemical exposure does not occur. If you are reading this book and find similarities to your own story, I pray you use it as motivation to make your own difficult choice. The choice to begin living a full life.

Contents

Introduction

Where does one begin when looking back on a life lived through the eyes and experiences of an alcoholic? What compels a person to even attempt in writing a story of his life when he struggles to remember most of it anyway? I've been praying on this concept and let's just say something finally clicked. Here follows the story of a guy who shouldn't have made it through life. Here is a story of a guy who is true living proof that God has a plan for each and every person. My story is much like every addict I have met during my life. We each have our own experiences of the same general rise and fall. One thing is for certain, though. We will all fall. The only main differences I see in the stories of addicts throughout the world is the individual's after life. I'm referring to life after the death of the active addict. Death to an active will leave his body in one of two conditions. This body will either be decomposing, cold and with a silent heart. Or, the body will be more beautiful than ever. The following chapters explain the journey of my body and soul as I experienced life as an active alcoholic.

The Early Years

A baby boy was born to a middle class, hardworking couple in the early 1980s. I remember my dad working hard with his business and my mom going back to school when I was very young. They both spent all their free time with me and eventually my younger brother. I was three years old when my parents came home with him and I wasn't very fond of sharing the attention. I wanted to please my parents and keep their attention on me. If I couldn't please them, I would act out and hope for the same results.

Preschool started for me when I was four years old. I hated it with a passion. Lucky for me though, I spent most of the next few years with my grandmother. No, nothing happened with my family. Both of my parents worked these years so I spent time with my grandmother from early in the morning and again after school. I quickly figured out how to play "hooky" and spend extra time with her. It was a regular occurrence to miss school and stay with her playing and watching television. I even got a bicycle during those years so I could ride it through town. It was a little town where everyone knew each other and there really wasn't any crime. We still lived in the generation where you could go out and play, but I knew to be back at their house as soon as the street lights lit up.

I was in a pageant and actually won my age group! I hated it, but it made my mother happy. Oh yea, I played the piano starting at the age of three and that made her really happy too. Although I'd miss playing later in life, I couldn't stand going to lessons as a child. Interesting stuff, I know.

Baseball was the other positive extracurricular activity I stuck with through most of my childhood. I loved playing ball like nothing else. My friends and I looked forward to playing our games and even practice 2-3 times a week. We were even excited to have extra time together while the dads hung out and drank beer at the ball park.

Pre-Kindergarten through sixth grade were good years in my childhood. I grew to become a chubby kid with good self-esteem, but low self-confidence. I always seemed to overdo things. Enough was never enough. I finished the bag of potato chips when I decided to have some. I also got straight A's in school when I decided to strive to achieve a high score. I was never the popular kid but I think more kids liked me than I thought. I never believed when someone complimented me because I never believed I deserved the compliment. "That was a beautiful piece you played at the recital this afternoon, Chip." My response, "I missed a key not two thirds of the way through the prelude." Why did I interpret these interactions with people as negative? I was very good at focusing on the negative aspects of everything, but I wasn't a negative or depressed child. Does that make sense? These years are my first true memories of my attitude. They are the first years of my actual memories. Do people usually have memories of their first 4-5 years without others telling them about it? I digress.

Seventh and eighth grades were somewhat awkward times for me. I got out and played with friends a lot more than earlier years. I felt awkward and unpopular though. I wasn't the best in sports so I didn't fully fit in there, but I didn't put all my effort in practice. I was scared and hated the exercise. I felt like my straight A's intimidated some of my classmates so I studied less. Neither of those things worked so I got aggravated. I started trying to fit in by showing off and having the coolest things. I put my efforts in begging my parents for the newest bike or the most in style clothes. That's what became most important to me. I still had the same feelings of enough isn't ever enough. My cravings were changing though. I was beginning to want more expensive items that my hard-working parents would struggle to afford.

11

They had my younger brother I mentioned earlier and had my baby brother during my eighth-grade year of school. I remember being excited to help them and feeling selfish at the same time.

I introduced myself to alcohol during this year. I remember being infatuated with the thought of drinking with all my family during a Christmas party my aunt would hold each year. I didn't have a peer pressure experience to make me want to try drinking. It was always readily available in my family's household so I just waited for them to let their guard down and I was able to get some myself. My first experience was with a whole lot of Goldschläger peppermint liquor. I remember sitting around a bonfire with my uncles and watching them have a good time. Then I remember lying in bed later that night with the room spinning and my parents coming in to ask me about my experience. "Are you dizzy or light headed?" my mom would ask. "Is the room spinning?" my dad would follow. "No, no I'm just tired." I would tell them, thinking I had them fooled. They had to know I drank alcohol that night after talking to me. It had to be obvious through swaying mannerisms and slurred speech. I'd lie about drinking alcohol every time after this moment.

The Teens

Oh, what emotional years for each and every person. You are beginning to venture out farther from your parents with a much longer leash. I know it was a very intimidating experience. My little school with classes of 25-30 kids per class suddenly grew to about 175 per class. My school merged with others in the area to form one local high school.

I wasn't ready for this. I didn't know how to cope. I couldn't see my friends nearly as much as I liked to see them and I found myself in classes with people I had never met before. I kept trying to play baseball and did make the team, but I'll get back to that later. I would spend most of my time riding ATVs through the country with my longtime friend. I was thirteen years old and living in the country so that summed up my social life. I was terrified of girls at school. Remember what I said about that low self-confidence? Yeah that decided to stick with me. I had a few sleep overs with friends so we could ride 4 wheelers through the night and stay up late playing video games or whatever else. I'd usually find my way in my parents' liquor cabinet, occasionally getting caught that night if my friends would have to wake my mom due to my being sick. I met a girl this year. Man, she really didn't know what she was in for when she let me in her life.

The night I met my first love...

It was a cool Friday night and I was at my high school's football game with my dad. I convinced him to take me so I could meet my friends. The parents always hung out in a certain little area of the bleachers and we had our own areas of the place to watch the game.   It gave us kids a sense of being there on our own. It also gave us some room where some of the older kids would sneak alcohol in and we would make some drinks as opportunity would allow. I saw this girl with her friends and I couldn't take my eyes off her. She was beautiful, but there was something about her that gave me the confidence to go over and talk with her. Well some alcohol in my young system and a long time of looking over her way with my friends picking on me may have had an influence. As I remember, I waited until the end of the game and asked for her phone number. She reluctantly agreed to give it to me, but neither of us had anything to write with. (See these were in the days you wrote numbers down on paper and called a girl's house.) I sealed the deal with a clever comment to her. "You're so beautiful, and I like you so much, I'll prove how much you mean to me already by remembering your number. I won't need to write it down." She smiled while I repeated every digit she spoke. We parted ways after that and I refused to forget that phone number.

I forget how long it went before I called. I do know that I was excited to talk with her but it took a little bit for me to gain the confidence. I thought I was much older and more mature than reality showed. I was a freshman in high school, a thirteen-year-old boy, working up the confidence to give a twelve-year-old eighth grade girl a phone call. We talked a few times after school but nothing would come of it for months.

The Spring months came around and baseball season started. I was a pitcher and we always started practice either late December or early January. With both of my parents busy with work and me having to stay late at school, I started riding home from school with older teammates. We were kids growing up quick! I saw myself as more of an adult than a child. I remembered the "to do" thing of having a beer after a long day. We would sometimes stop at local "hole in the wall" stores that would sell alcohol to us and indulge before going to the house.

I went out to a party for the first time at the end of my Freshman school year. My parents let me go out with one of my older teammates after I begged and pleaded with them. I remember getting alcohol at the store and the little Swisher sweet cigarettes. Man, I was feeling like I was ready to party with friends. *I don't remember anything else about that night!*

Summer time was filled with work around my family's property and baseball. Our league was good and we usually went to the parish and sometimes state tournaments. We loved out of town tournaments because it was always a party at the hotel. Adults would visit with each other while enjoying cold beverages and we would plan how to sneak some drinks. Most of the time, at least one of the teammates would have something stashed from home so we could "party".

The first day of my Sophomore year was an interesting one. Remember that girl I talked about earlier? Yeah? Well I saw her at lunch and she was facing away from me. I walked up behind her and told her she would be mine. She was surprised, but knew it was me behind her and we were soon inseparable.

First Time for Everything

We went out with a couple of my buddies one night to see a bunch of others partying at a bowling alley. I think we had been dating for about three months or so. It started off like any other night I was going out with friends, but my love was sitting in the back seat next to me. The usual stops were made in my little town to get drinks so we could get a buzz before going out. I was drinking heavy as usual but talked myself in to having a special reason this night. See the topic of sex came up on the way to the bowling lanes. I knew that I was the only one in the car that was a virgin so you can only imagine how I was a scared kid. Thoughts were racing! "What was going to happen?" "Do I make a move later?" "Will she?" "Where though?!?!" My thoughts went out of control. I did my best not to show it to my friends, but I don't think I hid my anxiety from Her. I don't remember if it was a Friday night or Saturday night, much less the date. I don't remember how we got started. I remember snap shots of our actions in the back seat of that car and I remember someone coming near the car to cheer us on for a minute. Next thing I remember was kissing her goodnight when dropping her off at home. My friend that drove us out had a celebratory drink with me on the way home from her house. We wrecked in a ditch when he went off the

road trying to hit a road sign with the pint
bottle.

We had plenty of good times that year. I had a girlfriend for the first time in my life and my older friends that had drivers' licenses would take us out every weekend. One in particular would be the guy driving us out most of the time. I don't remember when it was exactly, but it didn't take long for him to get tired of seeing us together in the back seat and rip the rear-view mirror off the car. I'll let you draw your own conclusions as to why that event took place.

My Junior year started off in an interesting way. I was looking like an adrenaline junkie by this age. Probably showed hints of it in my younger years, but my parents were supporting some of my habits by rewarding good grades and other achievements with 4 wheelers (ATVs) and go fast parts. I had a four-wheel drive ATV and a racing ATV. We lived out in the country and I was working on them, riding them, drinking, or all the above. Alcohol wasn't an everyday thing. I mostly drank on the weekends or maybe during the week if friends got together. I still didn't have my driver's license and felt a little left out most of the time.

Okay, back to the interesting start. A couple of friends were helping me paint a fence two weeks before school started. I had one ATV hooked to the little utility trailer and used my racing ATV to run back and forth to the house if needed. We worked for the majority of the day. I decided to make a quick ride around three or four o'clock that afternoon. I don't remember why I decided to get on that thing. I started it up and left the guys for a minute, went to the back of the property and turned around. I remember thinking I was going to "give it all its got" and show off. It was such a thrill riding this thing. I felt like I was always an inch from losing complete control. The ride was almost done and I was about one hundred yards from getting back to the guys when I lost control jumping over a levee. The bike sprung up so quick my only reaction was to jump up from it with as much power as possible. I remember being ten to fifteen feet in the air and watching the ATV hit the ground. The front end went down and it started flipping violently. Things seemed to be in slow motion at this point. I knew I was going to be next and prepared for my impact. The ground felt hard as rock. Parts of me felt an absurd pressure and went numb. Others burned as though I was on fire. My mind suddenly turned from slow motion to real time speeds. The fifty something foot slide and flip was quick and I was back on my feet. "I'm okay. I'm okay." I told myself as I patted parts of my body. Then I noticed I left a trail of shoes, a sock, and even my pants on the ground where I slid. That's when I looked down and noticed the entire area above each knee had third degree brush burn. If you're familiar with golf, it looked like I had two big divots on my legs. "Shit! Well at least its numb." I hobbled over to the start of the wreckage collecting my things and that's about the time my friends pulled up to me. They helped me inside the house and I experienced the most painful shower in my life.

It was difficult to walk for about a month after the accident. The burns got infected and I had to pour hydrogen peroxide on them to eat out the bacteria filled tissue. I kept gauze on them most of the time because if not, blood would seep through my khaki school pants. My girlfriend helped me through these times and I don't think I ever thanked her for it. If I did, it wasn't nearly enough.

As I healed up and started getting out more, my life got back to the same routine. My friends were on the football team. I didn't care to play high school football because I thought it would ruin my Friday night fun every week for half of the year. So, I would find a way to watch the games when they played at home. Then we would sometimes go to a party afterwards. Saturday nights were usually the big nights though. My friends with licenses would drive us out and we had a local country bar letting us inside at that point. If there wasn't a party, we would go to the bar all night. Drinking continued to be an every weekend thing and during the week as opportunity allowed. I'd get blackout drunk at least once a week and have to apologize to my girlfriend and best friend for something I did to them. They put up with me though. We all took it as something kids did during those years.

Springtime came around and I got involved with baseball again. This season began frustrating me from the very beginning. The Senior class was filled with talent. I was playing varsity ball. Ha, "playing" is a loose term. I was sitting the bench and quickly getting bored. My mind was playing out all the scenarios of how my days would be going if I wasn't sitting in a dugout. A group of us even found a store nearby that would sell us alcohol. My coach had a commitment immediately following last period so he pushed practice back to start a little over an hour after school ended. Oh boy! That's all the time we needed to get to this store and get something to drink. Our favorite drinks were Slush Puppies with Everclear 180 proof alcohol in them. I liked the large green apple with three to four shots in each one. Things went great from there now that I was showing up to ball practice with a buzz. I didn't think it affected my performance at all. I was just much more tolerant of knowing I was second string.

I quit playing almost half way through that season. I felt like coach would call me in to play at the worst of times. Coach catered to his golden boy seniors and I would only get playing time if we were ridiculously ahead or had no chance of winning the game. The third baseman, which is the position I played, started making errors in one game. My mind was on the mistakes. "Why isn't coach putting me in to replace him?" I was furious. I quit the next day. Coach actually explained to me why he didn't pull the starter and told me his plans for giving my chance to take the spot the next game. I didn't want to hear that shit. I didn't have the patience. I was ready to have my fun after school riding ATVs and doing whatever I wanted. I had friends that seemed to have so much fun after school. They were always running the roads or doing something, anything more interesting than what I was doing.

I cheated on my girlfriend that year. I don't remember her ever catching me, but she definitely suspected I was up to something. I went from spending all my free time with her to making excuses why I couldn't. Sad thing is the other girl lived just around the corner from her. I nearly drove by one house to get to the other. My best friend knew what I was up to but he didn't care. Bros first! He also fooled around with her best friend so we were both occupied most of the time. We skipped school together and hung out at one of our four homes while the parents were at work. We thought we were big shots. I knew that it wasn't something that would go anywhere. I knew she wasn't good for me, even though she was so hot! If you can believe it, my heart completely belonged to my girlfriend. See, I was so insecure that I needed validation. Why would anyone be attracted to me? I still thought I was fat and always built my self-confidence on material items. I took my girlfriend for granted. She must not have been able to get anyone else. I mean, why else would she want to be with me. I didn't realize she saw things in me I couldn't see myself. She saw my best character traits, things so good that they offset my faults. The fling lasted for a few weeks at best. My buddy and I were both dirty cheaters during this time period. The thrill was indescribable though. Drinking, sex, and other things without getting caught, Whoa! He and I both ended our flings at the same time. We couldn't do it separately because we were always double dating and covering for each other. We literally set my dad's dumpster on fire while burning Polaroid pictures of our excursions. You remember those? That wouldn't happen today since no one prints pictures anymore.

I got my first truck somewhere in the mix of all these events. I really don't remember exactly when it was that my parents bought it for me! Man, that's a shame. I remember events around having my truck. I fell in love with a particular vehicle an old man had up for sale and my parents bought it before I got my actual driver's license. It was an immediate love for me. I couldn't wait to start customizing it! It was also the beginning of trouble for me.

Summer before my senior year, I pulled a good one. My friend and I were hanging out one evening. There wasn't much to do so we decided to "ride around and drink". That meant we would load an ice chest down with beer and go to our spots we usually found people to visit. We were making stops at a few places when we found ourselves at the local car wash. A couple other people were hanging out there and we stopped to say hello. We really stopped to empty out the cans from the back of the truck. It started raining while we were tailgating over there. It was the first rain in at least a couple of months. As we were all car or truck guys, we picked on each other about whose vehicle was faster and more powerful. Keep in mind the roads were wet now. I was the second to last vehicle leaving and we were headed to a country bar where we would play pool and they sold us beer. I hardly made it out of the parking lot. We were showing off and I started spinning the tires as I pulled on to the road. I struggled to keep the truck straight as I steered right, left, right, left. I found myself with the wheel turned all the way to the right and my foot on the brake so hard I was trying to push the pedal through the floor. We slid several feet and made our way into the eight-foot-deep ditch on the left side of the road. The truck came to rest in almost three feet of water and was nearly turned on the driver's side. We climbed out and I got so scared. "What am I going to do? I'm 16 years old and been drinking. I'm going to jail!" The people around us ran over and we started brainstorming. "Call so and so with his four-wheel drive truck! He will get you out no problem!" I heard from behind me. "But I'm in town! There's no chance someone will pull me out before the cops get here!" Sure enough the officer in town passed by within a few minutes. He talked to me for a minute and to my surprise, he let someone attempt to pull me out. He had to know I was drinking because he requested someone else get in my vehicle while getting it out. I didn't question anything. I just followed orders. My parents showed up after a while, but this event turned in to a party by that time. They had to park two blocks away due to the number of spectators. I got off that night with no negative consequences, except for the disappointment of my parents.

The next day was fun dealing with the water damage in my truck. I began washing and airing it out. I was good at mechanics and took care of everything myself. I disassembled the interior and took the carpet out. I shampooed the carpet and cleaned the rest of the truck's interior while it dried. Later that day, it was looking and smelling better than before. I learned a lesson that day. "Don't be so aggressive with the throttle when the roads are wet!"

I started that senior year with such mixed feelings. My best friend was still there because we were in the same class. The rest of my friends, besides my younger girlfriend, had all graduated. I put as much emphasis on my ATVs and truck as I could because they were the only things I enjoyed, besides my lady and the demon on my shoulder. I experienced several nights where I'd put myself in a ditch and need to get pulled out. I'd miss the driveway at my house when coming home from a party or bar. I even let my younger brother get punished for "tearing up the front ditch with the four-wheeler". He didn't have anything to do with that. I went out the night before. It was wet and I missed the driveway. I corrected by turning in to it and somehow spun the tires back and forth a few times and was able to climb out. I hosed the truck off and parked in my usual spot. No one suspected it would have been me!

Another night worth mentioning during that year was a miracle of sorts. My buddy and I roamed the roads all day, drinking. It was a holiday, but I can't remember which holiday. We went from one social event to another and ended up at some older friend's house party. They were quite a few years older than us because they already had a house on their own, a young couple. Around ten or eleven o'clock that night, we got the bright idea to check out a bar that was having a special event. We drank over a case of beer that day already and weren't checking up. A couple of people at the party voiced concerns about us getting on the road but ended up just telling us to be careful. We backed out the driveway, did a little "burnout", turned up the radio system, and we were on our way. The twenty-mile drive was silky smooth. We had classic country screaming out of the open windows and echoing through the night.

When pulling up to the bar we both got the feeling our efforts were in vain. There were only a few cars in the parking lot and hardly anyone inside the place. Oh well, might as well have a beer while we are here. One or two beers and a game of pool later, we left to head back to our friend's party.

There was only one town between the bar and our friends' house we were driving back towards. Our timing was perfect. We turned on the only section of four lane road in the whole drive and end up behind a car. The car was driving the speed limit, but my boy didn't ever drive the speed limit. He decides to pass the car. It wasn't a violent acceleration or anything. He didn't want the loud exhaust I put on the truck to be heard and alarm any nearby police. What did he not realize? It was the town police he was passing. The only officer on duty and we decide to pull in the left lane, speed considerably, and pass him. Yeah, we got stopped right away. I don't think we made it all the way around him by the time he had his lights on. We were screwed. The bed of the truck was full of beer cans from that day and days prior. We had an ice chest with beer in it. We were seventeen and eighteen years old. We each had a plastic cup of beer in our hands because we had to get one for the road when leaving the bar, as if we didn't have any in the truck.

We were both panicking as we pulled over in that parking lot. I figured my friend was going to jail and maybe

I was too. He gave me his beer to hold as he stepped out of the truck, following the officer's orders. I could hear questions being asked. I heard my friend deny drinking. I heard the officer call him out while shining the flashlight in the bed of the truck. I heard the officer say "Well if your passenger isn't drinking, why isn't he driving?" "Fuck me, man!" I couldn't admit to drinking or I'd get arrested for being underage. I have two cups almost full of beer on the floorboard between my feet and I'm holding them so they don't spill. The office approached the driver's window since they were on that side of the truck and shined his light at me. He asked me to exit and show him my ID. I don't know why, but he backed away and back towards my friend before I got out my seat. God had to be with us that night. Somehow, I exited the truck without spilling the beers and made it over to where they were standing. I was sweating as I fumbled through my wallet. "You sure you aren't drinking, son?" he asked. "No Sir, I'm just very nervous. I haven't been stopped before." I replied. I was able to clumsily hand him my driver's license and he was looking at my information on it when he got a call. He got a call on his cell phone! I don't remember any more of his conversation than "All right! I'll be right there!" He was flustered over something when he handed both of our IDs back to us and said "You two be careful getting out of my town and go home." He pointed to my friend "You let him (me) drive and get your ass in the passenger seat!" The officer ran to his car that second and sped out of the parking lot. We stood there, looking at each other for a few minutes, baffled.

I drove the rest of the way through town. We were both silent and had the radio off. It was so awkward! A couple of miles out in the country, my friend finally asks to drive again. I pulled over, put the truck in park, and he handed my beer to me with a smile on his face. "Damn bro! That must have been one hell of a booty call, huh!" We both laughed as we switched places in the truck. We were back on our buzz, feeling like we could get away with anything. The music went back on and we continued our journey.

When we got back to the party, it was the talk of the night. They all tried getting us to realize how lucky we were, but we had already convinced ourselves we made a major accomplishment. We got away from the police. We did it.

Big Man on Campus

College was interesting, to say the least. I was seventeen years old and had no clue as to what I wanted to study in college. Both of my parents pushed me towards the medical field. Well, push may be a strong word. They urged me to pursue a career in the medical field due to stability and well paying positions. I wanted to build stuff. That's as far as I got!

I started out majoring in Electrical Engineering. Between the lack of enthusiasm for school and foreign professors I could barely understand, I was quickly skipping class. I wasn't doing anything crazy when missing class, I just didn't want to be there. Also, most classes were very large and professors didn't take roll. I could get away with a lot while having so much freedom. There was a breakfast and lunch spot where most students hung out while on campus. I enjoyed this place. The food was excellent and they had gaming tables. I felt like I was at a bar, minus the alcohol and smoke. Well, I brought alcohol from time to time so it was closer to a bar more times than not. It never bothered me that no one else was drinking. I was never asked questions about class either. Somehow, my grades were staying average. I'd also see plenty of my friends come and go while I was hanging out. I had different groups to chill with each hour of the morning.

My second semester included a change in course of study. I spoke with my parents and shared my lack of interest in what I was doing. My mom informed me I could study Pre-Pharmacy in Louisiana. I could figure things out while still taking my general studies classes and I didn't have to change schools. I could even go back to an engineering curriculum and wouldn't lose any time. It was an easy decision for me, especially since I just didn't know what I wanted to study. I even got a job in a pharmacy at the local hospital. I went "all in" with trying to figure out if that's what I wanted to do for the rest of my life. My mom's motto was "You can do all the things you like to do on your free time, with the money you make while working in a pharmacy. Career comes first." She was right with what she told me, but it wasn't what a hard headed eighteen-year-old wanted to hear.

I was back in an engineering curriculum the following semester and it was good stuff. I switched to more of a mechanical field. The classes were great and it peaked my interest. We were learning binary codes while designing small electrical systems. We designed hydraulic systems, pneumatic systems, and even started machining parts in the engineering workshop. I liked it enough to attend most of my classes and really start to excel in my group. We still did plenty of drinking and partying, but it was extracurricular. We planned parties or made it out to the strip where all the college students would go out. I especially liked going out on Wednesday nights because my girlfriend couldn't come since she was still in high school. It was a very popular night for the strip with outrageous drink specials. I'd go every chance I could. My only memories were showing up, though. Twenty-five cent bourbon and cokes are a mad recipe for offending every female around you and blacking out. Yes, I know I just mentioned my girlfriend. Yes, she was at home sleeping. Yes, I was hitting on college girls while out at night. I was a selfish, alcoholic eighteen-year-old, remember?

My second and third years of college were more of the same. I grew to love the curriculum I was in and spent more time in class and in the work shop. My classes were in the latter stages of an evolution from morning to afternoon. I kept scheduling them later and later so I didn't have to get up early for school, just in case I decided to go out or something. I used my work schedule as my excuse, but that wasn't really the case. I was still working evenings at the hospital pharmacy and usually got home around eleven at night.

My longtime friend and I started going to an off-road park a couple hours away from home. We started making weekends out of it. My girlfriend would come with me most of the time too. I still had my two ATVs so I always had a backup when I broke something on my racing bike. Also, I had that second bike to haul the ice chest full of beer! We would usually drink about a case of beer a day while at the park. That's a case of beer for each of us while camping over there. The days were spent racing with light drinking. The nights involved cruising to each other's camp sites and drinking until oblivion. I can't count the number of times one, or both, of us would pass out sitting on our bikes. We would usually make it to the tent or lay down on the trailer at some point, though. We got very lucky those years. I flipped my bike over a few times, nearly hit trees and other stuff. We witness other people crash and even helped while on a ride one night when a couple guys hit a fence. Paramedics relied on the two of us to get them to the scene of the accident and I even toted the injured rider strapped to a spine board on my rack. Things like this happened in my life and I never realized it could happen to me.

Back to life in college, I was excelling! The courses were finally getting to where they were specific to engineering practices and we started building projects. I brought my personal projects to school from time to time trying to show off. I always found excuses as to why I needed to show a professor something, but I was just hoping to get someone's approval. I didn't care whose approval I got, the attention is what I needed.

The fourth year of my college career was filled with changes. I found a job working in a local manufacturing facility as an apprentice. It was a fun experience working there as I was learning the entire operation. They allowed me to work part time around my school schedule and I started out in the fabrications shop. I was doing what I loved, even though it didn't pay me what the pharmacy tech job paid. I felt as though the knowledge I was gaining offset the pay. School progressed as well. My work and my studies were now in line with each other. I didn't go out as much through this time. I kept all activities involving alcohol and parties confined to the weekends. Some weekends didn't involve much of that either. My girlfriend from high school was now in college, too. The difference here is she was a three-hour drive away from me. We were fighting through a long-distance relationship. I know she had a tough time being away, but I feel like I took it harder than she did. I'd drink and cut up so I only imaged she was doing the same. I couldn't think how else anyone would act. It may not have been the case, but it was my reality.

We were broken up, maybe just "taking a break" for a while when I was involved with my fifth year of college. It came to be too much. I think it was pretty much all my fault. I couldn't handle things the way they were. Also, I finished my apprenticeship and quit the manufacturing company when they wouldn't increase my pay to keep working there full time. A welding shop just outside of town hired me at a competitive salary and I worked there for a few months. School kept going steady and my grades were getting better and better. Classes got more specific to my field with every passing semester. I was nearing the end of my Spring semester when that welding shop let me go. I was too naive to realize they hired me to complete a big project they had coming up. The contract had a strict deadline and they needed someone extra working in house to ensure it would be completed on time. That guy was me; however, I wasn't needed once it was done.

A couple weeks of being unemployed and out of school that summer, I was day drinking and messing around more than ever. Boredom and the feeling of uselessness overwhelmed me. The bottom of each bottle showed up well before any of my sorrows were drowned and just as I was giving up, I got a call. An oilfield rental company needed a contract welder/fabricator to build structural equipment. I couldn't wait to interview and the owner of the shop accepted a meeting the next day. We clicked immediately and I impressed him with my welding skills when I tested. I was back in the game! Ha! Not only was I back, but I was making more money as an independent welder than I ever made in my life.

Things were looking so good for me. I was building all sorts of things with this shop. The owner and I were the only two fabricators there and he treated me like an equal. We quickly became best friends as we worked. We also began hanging out after hours to have a few beers. I spent the rest of my summer with him. The extracurricular activities eventually showed me something very scary though. He was just like me. He was just like me in my alcoholism a few years in the future. And I was too happy to be going along for that ride.

We got to a point where I was meeting all of his clients so I could take orders from them and estimate build times. He was taking me to lunch with them, which I enjoyed. The bad side of that was alcohol being involved every time we went to lunch. We would eat and then drink beer for a couple of hours some days. There was even a place that had some of the best margaritas. We would get a good buzz from those things while discussing upcoming projects. Then we would head back to the shop and weld for the rest of the afternoon. It didn't work out all the time, though. We were both alcoholics so we didn't know how to stop drinking. He kept a fridge stocked at the shop. He would have to leave some days to get more as we were always drinking in between welds.

I worked there for a few months and then transitioned to running my own welding rig on the road. I was still doing business with the guy, but I spent much less time there. This was both my decision and his. We had a couple of days where we drank way too much together and I believe he knew we weren't good together, just as I did. We didn't "fall out" or anything, just started gong our separate ways. Welding on the road was good to me. I could charge a higher rate and I was able to start making money from a helper. I hired guys temporarily to give me a hand on job sites while making a profit on their hourly salary. Life was good. Also, working on site and in customers' yards meant I couldn't drink while working. I'd still drink on the way home after work, but it limited my opportunity severely. The time constraints were helping me get by, but I was still progressing in my alcoholism.

I started to show the arrogance and selfishness as I was now making more money. I went and bought a brand new four-wheel drive diesel pickup truck, brand new welding equipment, nice clothes, and all the things I knew I wanted to project success. I wanted guys to envy me and women to want to be with me. It worked, too. It especially worked around school. I'd get back to my truck after classes with notes on my window from girls that wanted to go out. I felt like I was on top of the game. Guys and girls alike would stare while I passed through campus on my way to the parking lot. It was more fun travelling to and from class than it was spending time on campus.

This period of time was the beginning of what I look back on as the highlight of my social drinking career. I was out drinking when I wasn't working or studying. I had plenty of dates and plenty of friends at the time. My phone rang constantly! The so-called friends I had were "moochers" though. They always wanted to go out with me because I'd pay the bar tab. We usually took my truck out so I was usually driving too. I was having so much fun. I blew money like there was no tomorrow. Young women were easy to come by as I was meeting them at school and seeing them out. A bunch of guys idolized me when we would go out to the bars because I'd get hugs and kisses every place we stopped. I was risking so much though. I'd work hard to control my drinking and did a good job of it most nights. I would have gone to jail for drinking and driving any night, so don't get me wrong. There was no designated driver. I just didn't get inebriated and that was a win for me.

Turns out I would find trouble on a night where nothing was going on. I wasn't at a bar or coming home from a bar. I worked in shop with the guy I mentioned earlier and it was a Friday so he had an ice chest ready for us before lunch. Some clients came over and grilled burgers with other stuff on the pit. We had cold beer for lunch and continued drinking until I left around four that afternoon. They were still drinking and making plans for that night when I left. I didn't plan to stop either. It was uncomfortable drinking and being that far away from home. So, I made it to the back roads and got comfortable. I switched to whiskey while cruising down gravel roads in my lifted truck. No one I knew was doing anything. Some were working late and others had things going on, it still didn't stop me. After driving several miles through the country, I was getting to the outskirts of town and only about five miles away from home. I was at the point where I barely remember the event, but a mustang came traveling towards me. Our vehicles made contact on each front driver's side, causing me to stop where I was and put them in the ditch. No one was hurt in the event, but my life would be changed. The police showed up and started assessing the scene. They were dealing with a head-on collision on a road with no center lines. The road surface was filled with gravel and pot holes. The driver of the other car didn't have a license. Things were looking as though we would each take our losses and go home, until they interviewed me. Yeah, I went to jail for drinking and driving. I was anxious, nervous, scared, an emotional wreck. They processed me and I passed out. My parents bailed me out of jail the next morning and all the unbearable conversations would soon follow.

I went through all of the legal processes involved with that charge. It cost a few thousand dollars and it was expunged. The interesting thing was counselors and instructors involved with the courses I attended during this process all told me they genuinely believed I just had a stroke of bad luck. I was twenty-two years old and was already manipulating people in believing I didn't have a drinking problem. Looking back, it's amazing how lying and manipulation comes so natural to the alcoholic.

The incident scared me straight for a little while. I never stopped drinking, but I wouldn't drink if I knew I'd have to drive home. As the days turned to weeks and then months, I became brave again. It was around that time I started having a couple of beers with the guys at work before leaving to go home. Or I would stop by the store and get something to drink. It didn't take long before I almost got in trouble again. I let the guys convince me to go out one Friday as we were finishing up with work. I already drank a couple beers, so I was easily persuaded when one of them offered for me to borrow clothes and stay at his place. Everything was good while starting the night out. I stuck with drinking beer and paced myself. I rode with one of the guys and I left my truck at his house, no big deal. We rode to a couple different bars until finally settling down at a place where he knew almost everyone there. Meanwhile, I tried to keep up with where we were, but I was lost. That shouldn't have mattered because I wasn't driving. I mention all of this because it did matter. The guy driving got stupid drunk from mixed drinks and shots while I was preoccupied shooting pool and visiting with other people in the place. Some people from behind the bar came get me before midnight and said we had to leave. They said I had to get my friend out of there, but were nice enough to offer to help. I asked a couple of others about giving us a ride and no one would drive. They all told me about how I was straight and should just drive him to his house. They gave me directions and I remembered the rest. I thought I had it, up until I got broadsided on the driver's side while exiting the parking lot. I didn't see a car coming from the left as I attempted to pull onto the highway. We got hit and pushed in a seven-foot ditch. My friend was lying in the back seat, uninjured. I had a burn on my arm from the airbag. We were lucky as the driver of the other vehicle left in an ambulance. Somehow, I was never tested or accused of drinking. Multiple witnesses from the place we were leaving testified on my behalf and that was that. We got a ride back to his place. Things didn't stop there for me though. I was so pissed about the whole situation; I got in my truck and drove home from his house. I drove over an hour to get home and arrived about four in the morning. I prepared the largest mixed drink I could and drank it in bed, eventually passing out while a movie played on television. No one besides the people at the incident knew what happened that night.

That incident didn't rattle me. Some things about the other driver came out and he was put in the wrong. I quickly forgot that I drank prior to that event and could have been arrested. The alcoholic mind does a very good job of forgetting what it doesn't want to know and concentrating on what it needs to justify its actions. I was back doing the same stuff the following weekend. To make things worse, my mind was convincing me I learned from the events so it couldn't happen again.

This puts me at the beginning of my last year of college. I was welding only on my own and on the road at this point. I made myself a portable welding rig that dropped in the back of my truck and I was set up. I'd drive to school in the morning, stay there until noon and then head out to job sites and work until late at night. I continued my same social life when I could, but work and finishing school was my top priority. I also met a girl in one of my classes that proved to be special to me, at least for a while. She made me work for our first date, too. We had good times in class together one semester and that was the only time she would see me or talk with me. It wasn't until the last week of the semester; she gave me her number and expressed interest in going out with me. I was ready! And her timing was good. That was the end of my very last full time scheduled semester and I had time to go out more. We were dating immediately. The first date went well and things moved quick. I didn't mind though, I was missing that part of my life. This girl wasn't the dinner and a movie kind of girl though. She was in her early twenties and ready to go any night of the week. She also lived with a gorgeous roommate in a quaint little townhouse. I'd regularly take them both out, sometimes with another friend of hers. Yeah, I felt like I was "the man" when going out with them. Funny thing is they knew what they were doing and exaggerated everything when we were at the bars. I had a beautiful girl holding on to each of my arms and they would all give me kisses. It wouldn't ever go further than a good show to make other guys jealous, but it sure went far enough to boost my ego. That fun relationship lasted for a few months before things changed. My ex-girlfriend from high school and through the years returned home. We got back in touch with each other and there was just something about her. I knew she was good for me.

That final semester brought many changes for me. I leased a shop and started producing products there, as well as on the road. I only had one class left to graduate. It was scheduled on Monday evenings, leaving the rest of my time for work. I was finally able to work full time, putting more effort in my career and relationship. We had rough times getting back together, but ultimately fell back in to where we left off. Things were never really bad between us. I'd act out at times while drinking and that's usually when we would split up. We shared a strong love for each other, which was never the problem. The history of breaking up multiple times and the baggage we were collecting along the way were wearing both of us down. Despite these obstacles, we still wanted to be together.

I soon found myself in an apartment, living with my girlfriend. We were settling down together. She was working while finishing college. I was a class away from graduating and my business was starting to pick up. Life seemed to be on track for us as marriage and long term plans started becoming increasingly common in daily conversations. Something was happening during this time, though. It took months to go bad, but it was inevitable. I got to a point where I was drinking too much in the evenings at home. My girlfriend wasn't asking me to stop completely, but she was watching close as I drank at night. She just didn't want me to get drunk out of my mind. I struggled, but I would do my best to stop drinking after one or two with dinner. She was okay with that amount, but it wasn't enough for me. I eventually started drinking before leaving my shop. My strategy was to drink a few before getting home, so I could have the same amount at the apartment while preventing an argument. She would witness me drink the same amount and I would get the buzz I wanted. The big problem was my progression. I started drinking more and more at the shop. The excuses came easy to me as I wanted to stay there and work on things while drinking. I wasn't fooling anyone though. I would get home late and already drunk half of the time.

Things took about a year to get this bad and a change was coming soon.

She came to the shop one day and wanted to make plans for a date that coming Friday night. I went along with her and promised to set plans. Honestly, I didn't put much effort to listening though. In fact, I remember her coming later in the afternoon when I should have been getting ready to close the shop and go home. Instead, I had several guys there drinking beer with me. We were playing around and working on one of the many projects I had at the shop.

Date night came quick and I didn't put any effort in making plans. I got as far as telling the guys I needed to leave the shop on time that afternoon. Well, we decided to all get lunch together and I thought a beer would be good with lunch. Yeah, that beer turned into three and I didn't make it longer than an hour at the shop before popping the top once again. We turned our attention to one of my projects that afternoon and I soon lost track of time. My girlfriend called me and I answered the phone while still unaware of the time. She was so frustrated and upset with me as she asked why I wasn't home. I thought it was around five thirty or six o'clock and reacted under that assumption. We argued for a minute and she told me not to worry about leaving and getting home because she wouldn't be there. She called her friends and decided to go out with the girls instead of waiting for me. We ended that call, both upset with each other. I looked at the time to see it was seven thirty. She had every right to be upset with me. She knew what I had been doing at my shop. Nothing stopped my stubbornness, though. I quickly made plans of my own. I knew that I needed to give her an hour to make sure she was gone from the apartment. I planned to go home at that time and get ready to go out too. She specifically told me that she was going out downtown and did not want to see me. So, my buddies and I were going out to our favorite bar on the other side of town.

We got to the place between around eleven o'clock and it was getting full. We liked this particular bar because it was toned down for the majority of the night, but things would always get interesting after midnight. The place stayed open later than all other bars so people would flock to it later in the night. This particular Friday night was going well for all of us. We had a group of five guys and were sitting back drinking beer and visiting, until the crowds starting getting there. I ran in to a couple of women I knew from college. We hugged and started catching up while having drinks. That didn't take us very long and we were soon cutting up on the dance floor. We were all drunk by this time and had little reservation. They were flirting with me and I loved it. The two would dance on each other and even kissed. I was a bit shocked when that happened but didn't have time to think much about it. One of them grabbed me and kissed me, then the other. I felt like I was in a movie or something! This could not be happening. Shit got real when I looked over to see my girlfriend staring at me. Yeah, it was real. I made an excuse to walk away from my friends and try to talk with her, but she wasn't having it. She left the place. "She wasn't even supposed to be there!"

My buddy and I rushed home to try and do damage control. Nope. That wasn't happening. My girlfriend was there and had her friends with her. It was over. She didn't want to see me at all. And I didn't make much of a plea in defense of my case. I turned to my phone and called one of the women I was fooling around with that night. She didn't live far from me and was happy to have me over. I left the apartment and headed to her place as my girlfriend and her friends watched me drive away. She didn't know where I was going or when I would be back.

Over at the other woman's place, we visited for a little while and put on a movie just for background noise. We were both tired and drunk. She was quick to let me know that I was not getting lucky just because I wanted to spend the night at her place. I was okay with that because I really just needed a place to stay. We kicked back in bed and got five minutes in the movie before she was on top of me. "Guess she changed her mind!" The following hours took my mind off what was going on at home. It wouldn't be until I was stepping in my truck the next morning, reality hit me. I had to go back to the apartment and face the finalization of my relationship. I didn't care at the time. The meaningless sex I had hours prior to picking up belongings from my ex proved I wouldn't be missing out on anything. Relationships meant consistent sex to me. And I was proving myself right by finding other women willing to take their clothes off with me.

Life Moves On

I spent a few nights with family and quickly found myself another apartment. I even decided to have a roommate since I was single and it would help both of us out. A friend of mine was looking for a place at the time and he needed a roommate to split rent. He was always stopping by my shop and drinking beer in the afternoons. We went out together sometimes on the weekends. We got along and it seemed like a great idea.

My living situation went from resembling married life to backtracking in early years of college. My roommate was several years younger than me. I wanted to be further along in life, but my actions were immature and I spent every dollar as soon as it was in my possession. I couldn't afford anything for the apartment and I didn't have much interest of buying things for the place. I spent all my time at my shop or out drinking. My bedroom was just nice enough for me to lay my head at night and support the occasional one night stand. I was good with those conditions.

A few months in to living the single life brought someone special into the picture. One day, a car pulled up to my shop and a beautiful woman stepped out. She had auburn red hair, big blue eyes, and the sexiest figure I ever saw. I stopped what I was doing and lost my train of thought. I couldn't think of anything besides that woman! "Who is she? Is that a potential customer?" "No, no, no, that's my sister bringing me lunch." One of the guys said as he walked out towards her. "Oh damn. I am not going to be able to help myself." I struggled to get my mind back on my work.

She showed up again the next morning, this time providing her brother with a ride to work. I waved and briefly acknowledged her while working on things in the shop. We went about getting work done and didn't say much about her, but the guy made subtle statements about how she was in a relationship and looking to be married in a year or so. I picked on him about it but I didn't put much thought in to my words or future actions. Well, I say that. She got to my shop to pick him up that afternoon and I decided to introduce myself. She and I seemed to get along well and I was most definitely attracted. I tried to respect her as I knew she was in a relationship, but subtle flirting couldn't be helped. She drove her brother to and from work a few days and then I was asked to pick him up. He didn't live far from my shop so I didn't mind. I was doing it more for her though. I was motivated by the chance of seeing her and maybe getting some brownie points by helping her out.

My worker started inviting me to stay over for a while in the evenings. I considered him a friend as well. We visited after hours at times and did some off-roading together. Hanging out at his house provided the time necessary for his sister to see me and get to know me. She had my phone number out of necessity. Her brother was difficult to get a hold of at times so she would call me looking for him. A couple of weeks after we met, she began calling me and texting me just to talk. We kept things quiet because she didn't want to be judged. She didn't want her family upset with her as she felt pressured in her current relationship. I was okay with whatever she asked me to do. I was smitten.

We talked and flirted with each other and the day finally came when we discussed going out on a date. She still hadn't gotten out of her relationship. It was such an awkward conversation at first as I was telling her about how much I wanted to do something together, but didn't want to push her away. She agreed after I summarized our night together. "Let's go watch a movie. It's not a date, just a couple of friends going to watch a movie. You can come to my apartment to pick me up and we will go straight to the cinema. No dinner or romantic stuff, just the movie. Afterwards, you can drop me back off to my place and go home. We can talk things over tomorrow."

She did just that! Our date, or whatever you want to call it, went just about the way I described it to her. There was a big difference towards the end, though. She got out of the car and came in my apartment with me after the movie. We went straight to my room and fooled around for a while. We stopped short of sex as she wanted to officially end her relationship first. Everything seemed to be going perfectly. See, I played in to the idea of wanting to wait. It was usually an angle that helped me out with women.

The next day proved a lot to me. She went through with ending her relationship and let me know she wanted to pursue a relationship with me. I was ecstatic! It had been a few months of living life single and doing my thing. That was enough for me as I felt like I found what I was looking for in that beautiful woman. She was working, independent, going to school to be a nurse, beautiful, and sweet on me. We didn't have any bad history and I didn't have to watch what I drank around her. We started our relationship with a clean slate.

Things were great for a while. The beginning of our relationship, before we told anyone we were dating, was especially good. I was her "safe place". She would escape from her troubles and no one would bother us while we spent time together. We needed these first few months together without intervention. We needed it more than I realized. I had no idea our relationship wouldn't be well received by the people around us. Her brother was one of the people that didn't want to see us together. The lack of acceptance angered me beyond reason. Looking back, some people had every right to be upset for her. Her brother was with me when I went out. He witnessed the failure of my previous relationship. Better yet, he witnessed me cutting up for months after that relationship failed. My bouts with women, alcohol, and continuous displays of immaturity were clear in his eyes. "It takes one to know one" is such a clear statement when dealing with addicts. She and I had a very strong bond by the time this resistance was felt. We were already sleeping together and confiding in each other. She was around me enough to see the great person I truly was, but not enough to continually witness the horror my drinking would bring about. I controlled my drinking around her for a long time. At this point, it only got away from me on a couple of instances when we were out at the bars. Between that and her blind love for me, she didn't believe what anyone said about me.

Things started turning bad as I got more and more comfortable with her. I got to a point where things annoyed me everywhere. I'd take anxiety from work back home with me. I'd take stress caused from my actions at home to work with me. The vicious cycle would repeat daily. My only escape was to drink myself to sleep every day. She began witnessing more of these addictive symptoms as she was staying with me more than ever. I was beginning to lose friends; my business was beginning to fail as work was getting slow. I was arguing with my roommate all the time. She stuck it out with me, though.

Before I move on, I need to elaborate on this. I was on the way to meet my girlfriend for a concert one night when an elderly lady ran a red light, broadsiding me. I called her immediately to let her know what was going on and she headed my way. No one was seriously injured in the accident. The police never checked me for drinking, luckily. I had a few beers before leaving work and a couple mixed drinks while getting dressed at the apartment. Witnesses stopped and gave reports to verify the lady was in the wrong. All I had to do was wait for copies of the paperwork and let the wrecker take my truck to the yard.

My girlfriend asked me what I wanted to do afterwards and I replied. "Let's go to that concert and I want a whiskey on the rocks." Alcohol was my cure all and she had sympathy for me that night. She drove us to the concert and kept a drink in my hand all night. Needless to say, I don't remember leaving the show.

I was back living in reality the following week. I had a rental truck from my insurance while the adjusters drug their feet with figuring out if my truck was totaled. I wasn't so worried about it while I had a nice truck to drive. We were approaching the Christmas holiday anyways and I had other things on my mind. December was always slow for my line of work and that was especially true this year. I was still okay financially, though. So, I took my free time and decided to spend it with my family and girlfriend. This was our first Christmas holiday together and we were both nervous. Nervous because of the tension our relationship caused, mostly amongst her family. We talked things through and came up with a plan. Christmas Eve would be spent with my family, and then we would go over to her family's gathering the next day. It seemed to be a solid plan and we figured the holiday would solidify our relationship.

Everything was going to plan as the holidays arrived. My girlfriend got to my apartment and visited with me while we finished getting ready. We loaded up my rental truck with presents and headed out to my parent's house. Christmas Eve was always a holiday my family cherished. I behaved myself and showed good face that night while some drank more than others. I had a couple of small drinks when we got there, but I stopped so I could drive home. My girlfriend had several whiskey drinks that night and I didn't mind one bit. I knew she was nervous. We all exchanged presents and we went back home around eleven that night. I dropped her off to her house and went back to my apartment. That's where I lost control. I was unloading my truck in an empty apartment as my roommate was with his family for the holidays. I was almost finished when I got to the bottle of whiskey I received from a cousin of mine. I turned on the television and sat back with a drink. The idea was to only have one while watching a little bit of a movie before falling asleep. I behaved all night and wanted to reward myself, and I did. I fell asleep a couple of hours later, after drinking the whole fifth of whiskey.

The next day came in what felt like moments. I woke up to a rhythmic pounding on the door and my phone ringing in the background. It was after one o'clock in the afternoon on Christmas day. My girlfriend was at my door, upset and worried. I was disoriented and unaware of what was happening at the moment. It took fifteen minutes or so for reality to set in and I suddenly realized what happened. I drank that bottled and passed out, causing me to miss her family gathering. I quickly showered and dressed while she waited, then we went to see her family. The people still there were nice. My absence that morning wasn't spoken about much. We never addressed what happened that day.

Shortly after that Christmas, my roommate and I had a falling out. He was getting tired of witnessing my alcoholism first hand. We would go out together and he would get the complete cycle from start to finish. I'd usually pass out in random places around the apartment. The final straw was pulled when I wrecked a truck he let me borrow. He was doing me a huge favor when my rental truck allowance from insurance ran out. I was someone he shouldn't have been helping. I was drinking almost every day and the amounts were getting to be more significant. The accident occurred about a mile away from our apartment in the middle of the day. I rushed to throw empty bottles out of the truck before people could see what I was doing and somehow never got questioned about it. I got a simple ticket for the incident and got a ride back home. The bad part of the event was my roommate only had liability insurance. My shop was failing at this time and I was looking to start a new career. He ended up absorbing all the loss on the truck and half of the cost for us to get out of the apartment. I somehow convinced my girlfriend it was a good idea for us to move in together. We found an apartment in the same complex and moved in as quickly as we could, but her family was not happy.

> *The day of that accident marked a significant event for me. I thought of suicide for the first time. My girlfriend stayed up with me that night while I cried uncontrollably. I was so scared of the upcoming repercussions. The arguments with my roommate and fear of losing her were both unbearable. I lost a friend, proved myself undeserving of receiving help, and turned to more alcohol to deal with the pain brought on by alcohol. That girl kept me company on the phone all night and our conversation kept me from acting on those thoughts.*

This also marked the beginning of the end for us. She was finally able to see what it was like to live with a selfish alcoholic. I took a class to keep me busy during the day so I could only drink at night. This helped me control the amounts of alcohol I drank. I started the habit of sneaking a drink in at home before going in to the apartment. The shop wasn't an option for me anymore and I was scared to get caught drinking and driving. Sitting in my truck and having a drink was the only way I could think of sneaking it in. My mind was going back to thinking it was the quantity she witnessed me drink, instead of the actions drinking brought about. I was blinded of the truth and had no idea what I was like once the substance took full effect.

She would leave to visit with her family some evenings. I used those opportunities to sneak extra drinks instead of realizing those actions were specifically why I wasn't there with her. She couldn't have me around her family when I was drinking. They didn't want to see it. I was an embarrassment.

We managed to stay in our relationship, regardless. It's crazy how long women stayed in my life! "Was I that good at manipulation? Did they have that much faith in me? Did they see glimpses of a truly beautiful person?" I may never know these things, but I have had several relationships that should have ended much sooner than they did.

The summer came around and I took my sweetheart to the Virgin Islands for a vacation with some family and other couples. I looked in to ways I could extend our trip for a little more intimate time and flights from New Orleans were my solution. I scheduled our flights and made hotel arrangements for the nights before and after our trip in the islands. This was a sure way to give us a little longer vacation. We did our own thing in New Orleans for a day and enjoyed a date night. I seemed to continue providing enough good times for her to put up with the bad, sort of. The trip started off great. We were enjoying ourselves and experiencing more "Firsts" together. Neither one of us had been to these islands. It was our first real vacation together, too. We shared such good times over that week. I was able to control my drinking to a point where I embarrassed myself twice out of the seven days. Both situations occurred when I drank the 80-proof rum instead of the 40-proof stuff. See, we started drinking before noon each day and continued until bed time. That meant the others would have a drink or two during brunch, then another few drinks later that evening. It meant consistent drinking for eight to twelve hours for me. It all depended on how long I lasted and I lasted longer than I remembered most days. I found myself apologizing for things I said or did without knowing what I was apologizing about. It's difficult to be sincere when you weren't mentally present during the actions. I must say, there was always a strange sense of sincerity that overwhelmed me, though. I subconsciously knew something happened. I argued with my girlfriend about my drinking towards the end of the trip. She told me some comments were made while I was drunk one of the nights and it pissed me off when I heard what was said. A couple of people over there with us voiced a concern for her having to deal with my drinking. That's all that was said. Something to the extent of, "Think about whether or not you want to deal with that alcoholic behavior. You have been together for a long time and have to be looking at possibly taking the next step." After I got over the initial defensiveness and softened up, she calmed down as well. We made up and I made more promises to quit my drinking. I think I was starting to believe myself. Maybe that's why I seemed so sincere in my pleas for her sympathy. We stopped over in New Orleans again at the end of our trip. It was even better this time. We had a nice dinner and spent quality time together.

Into the Deep Blue

I accepted a new position a few weeks after that vacation. I had been working towards this new endeavor and the opportunity finally presented itself. I was going offshore! A new program was kicking off at my company and I was chosen as one of the guys to spend a few weeks training before getting a rig assignment. It was a very exciting time for us. I was looking at long term relationship goals with my girlfriend and was concentrating on offshore work to provide financial stability. It was new and exciting for me.

Training kicked off and that time was nice. It provided me with the same work schedule as my girlfriend. We hadn't ever had that before. I lived at my shop when I was self-employed and worked mostly evening and night shifts after closing the shop down. This was refreshing and frustrating at the same time. I found myself fighting urges to drink and usually downing a half pint to pint of whiskey somewhere in the parking lot of the apartment complex. I repeated this behavior over and over. The only thing that kept me from drinking more every evening was spending time with her at home. The accountability of work first thing in the morning helped control my drinking some, but

I'd always push it when I had the chance. I went out with coworkers a few times and drank more at home if my girlfriend went to visit with her family. I wasn't in a good place.

Somehow, I made it to my first offshore assignment. This would mark the beginning of a successful career for me. It also provided me with a work and living environment free from alcohol. I knew it, even at that time. I still remember the first time heading out. I was scared, excited, nervous, you name it. The helicopter flight left early on a Tuesday morning and I was hungover from drinking the night before. I drank as much as I could stomach the night before. "When is the next time I will be able to enjoy a drink? I'll be offshore for weeks!" That didn't seem like such the great idea while sitting on an uncomfortable seat of the helicopter, wedged between a couple other guys. I was fighting motion sickness with nausea brought on with the aftermath of a binge.

I arrived mid-morning, on board a floating structure I had never been able to picture in my imagination. It was flat and had a tall structure towards the back. It was full of equipment I had only read about in books. The first steps on board were a bit chaotic. Imagine departing a helicopter on board a steel structure as it sways with the motions of ocean waves while the rotors are still spinning above you. I was in awe while trying to remember all of the procedures of rig embarkation taught in the classroom.

My mentor was waiting for me under the helideck and eager to meet me. He seemed like a genuine guy from the start. We visited briefly and he began walking me through the steps. First, I was to sign the log sheet and go through an onboarding process. After that, we would be meeting back up and he was going to take me on a short tour of the interior of the vessel while introducing me to rig management. I remember most of the details of this day. It stands out as one of the most important days of my life. I even met some of the most influential people I'd know in my life. Some would eventually become longtime friends, others would have "falling outs" with me.

Time seemed to speed up and slowdown in the various moments of that day. I had so much to learn and absorb while experiencing the absolute beauty of being out in the ocean. The rig operations made noises I never heard before. There was also a constant background noise, a "humming" or "groaning" of sorts. The engines provided those sounds while the thrusters added vibrations of varying intensities as they fought sea currents.

My mentor finished giving me the first tour of the place and it was soon time for bed. I was able to make a brief call to my girlfriend and my first day was done. What a day! And I was exhausted, both mentally and physically.

My second day proved to be much better as I woke up without a hangover. I stuck to my mentor's side and observed as he showed me how to function in my role. I stayed as an observer only for about a week, which passed by all too quick. He decided I was starting my second week by sharing the duties and responsibilities of the position. I was petrified, talk about getting out of your comfort zone!

I was fortunate for a mentor to push me like he did. He recognized my talents and forced me to be uncomfortable while supporting my success. (If you have any experience with recovery and working with a sponsor, you should experience the same.) The end of my fourteen-day hitch arrived and I was presented with a surprise. We were placing our bags in the waiting area, preparing to go home when I was notified the night guy coming out was turned away from the heliport. I was two weeks offshore, two weeks sober, and alcohol was still affecting my life. Well, I say alcohol. The truth is it may have been drugs, I never got a confirmation. A random drug and alcohol screening was given to all workers crew changing at that particular heliport. The guy that was coming out to work nights in my position refused to take the drug and alcohol test. His refusal was automatically counted as a positive, preventing him from flying offshore and ultimately getting him terminated. Now with all that being said, I was offered the night position. It was an opportunity I could not refuse!

I grabbed my bags and went back to bed after thanking my mentor and rig management for having faith in me. Of course, I couldn't sleep during that day and anxiously awaited the night. I was going to be sitting in the main seat of our office and running the show myself. The manager working nights with me was amazing, too. He helped coach me in every way he could. He was a friend to me, one that I would keep for years. I even had time to spend more time on the phone with my girlfriend in the evenings. We talked about how well I was doing at work. We talked about how everything was going at home with her schooling and work. Things seemed to be going in the direction I wanted and I could see success in our future. Two weeks of working the night shift put me at my limit of consecutive days spent offshore and it was time for me to get home for a few days. I got permission to go home for only four days to "reset my clock" before returning offshore. My managers and mentor agreed to continue training me during the day while he was on the rig even though I was already working on my own.

Crew change day finally came around for me and it was time to go home! The excitement of my new career was keeping me occupied offshore, but I sure did miss my love. I missed my girlfriend too. Ha! Okay but really. I consciously missed my loving girlfriend more than anything. My subconscious had me at the store buying a bottle of alcohol before I ever got home. Please understand that put me drinking a whiskey and coke around nine o'clock in the morning. I stopped to surprise her at work with whiskey on my breath and I didn't even realize what I was doing.

I continued home and continued drinking through lunch that day. I stopped after lunch, but I had also been awake since the previous afternoon. Needless to say, I fell asleep on the couch and only remember seeing my girlfriend awake that night for a minute while transferring from the couch to the bed. "Tomorrow will be better; I will make it up to her tomorrow." I remember my thoughts as I fell asleep once again.

The next morning came quickly and I made sure to wake up early with my girlfriend. I made coffee and breakfast so we could eat together before she had to leave for work. She didn't really say anything about my actions the night before so I figured I got away with it. I figured she didn't mind me sleeping through the evening after being away for a month. "Well she knows I worked nights the past two weeks, maybe she understands what I'm going through." I truly believed those thoughts as they ran circles in my mind.

That day and the next were good days. I stayed true to my word and didn't let her down. I don't think I let her down. I stuck to only a pint or so during the day and managed not to drink around her. We had a date one night and stayed in the next. We even made love both nights. I was once again feeling great about our relationship and where we were going. My last night at home brought me back to reality as I drank enough to black out that evening. I remember us having good times at home and even playing around in bed. It couldn't have been that good, though. I barely remember it. I left the apartment to head back offshore the next day after being home for four days. I drank all four days and got drunk two of them. My conscious was guilty and filled with regret as I drove to the heliport.

Time on the rig seemed to keep on passing by as I was continuing to enjoy what I was doing. I had the self-fulfillment of helping people as part of the new career. My relationship at home seemed to be continuing in a downward spiral. I was setting us up for financial success, earning an offshore salary. I was making up for not being present while home, my lack of presence all together. I spent my three months offshore with less than a week at home. This three-month period was great for my sobriety and gave my girlfriend the freedom she needed. My friends started telling me she was going out with other guys. I didn't want to believe them at first, but pictures were sent to me as evidence. We were done, it didn't matter what kind of money I thought I was giving to make up for my shortcomings. She made up her mind and gave up on me.

Of course, I wasn't going to be at fault for the failure of our relationship. I was easily able to concentrate on her time cheating on me. I made my plans while offshore and without confronting her about what she was doing. I wasn't going to be left, I was leaving! There are no winners with relationships involving active addiction, just sadness.

Tale of Two Lives

My return home from the rig involved packing and financial changes to accounts. I had to protect my money before it was too late. The stuff in our place could stay with her, I didn't want it.

I had everything finished by lunch time. I told her I was back and asked her to come home for lunch. She did and walked in to the place without a clue of what I did that morning. I briefly confronted her and we both got emotional. I think she was angry and I was sad. I felt heartbroken because I had already convinced myself I had no blame in the situation. The truth didn't matter at the time as I just needed to relieve myself of blame. The whole event didn't take twenty minutes and we were both out of the door. We agreed to spend the weekend apart and consider talking again after the weekend. I held back tears until I got in my truck. My memory does not tell me if she had tears as well.

As I left the apartment complex with a truck packed with clothes, I called a friend. "What the hell is going on this weekend? I need to get away and have some fun!" He told me about a party on South Padre Island. I was in the mood for spontaneity. "Hell Yeah! I'm on the way!" I managed to realize where the island was located once it was put in my GPS. "Shit......Fuck it, I'm still going!" Thoughts of my relationship and next moves raced through my mind as I began the first minutes of a twelve-hour drive.

South Padre was different than any other place I had been before. The party started soon after we arrived that night and the drinks flowed smooth. I saw people I knew from years before and met new ones from all through Texas. That night was a blur as I was exhausted and quickly drunk. I do remember hitting it off with several women at the place that night. Something about a Cajun accent those Texas girls could never resist.

Everyone kicked off the next morning as normal car show stuff went. (Oh yeah, it was a car and truck show/party going on that weekend.) My friend and I piled in his truck with a couple of girls. We were sipping beer that morning while nursing hangovers. A day at the show was hot and the beach was a nice break that afternoon. My interesting time of the weekend showed when everyone was going to a club on the island for the Saturday night party. One of the girls stayed in the room with me to finish getting ready and we connected. Both of us were just getting out of relationships and were trying to escape.

We decided to stay in the room while we had it to ourselves. Proved to be a good time! There was something to be said about letting out frustrations on one another that night. She and I were talking over drinks when I found myself caught in the most intense intimacy of at least a year. Afterwards was filled with more drinks and talking about how neither of us wanted to catch up with the others. The party was of no interest.

She brought up the idea of driving back home that night. She offered to drive my truck and give me a few hours to sober up before needing to get behind the wheel. I was convinced enough to get the drive over with already. We each felt as though our needs for the weekend were met. Neither of us wanted to continue the weekend facing others in our group and dealing with questions. We were on our way shortly after midnight, headed to Houston.

I slept almost the whole way to Houston as we got to her place shortly after eight in the morning. It was a quick goodbye with a brief hug and kiss on the cheek. Now sitting behind the steering wheel, I needed to figure out how to get home to Louisiana. I pulled in to a nearby gas station and picked up a couple soft drinks while looking over the map and setting my GPS. I commenced to make myself a drink with whiskey left over from the night before, but it was for later down the road. I just didn't want to stop again.

Yeah, that drink was supposed to last longer than an hour in to the drive. A phone call from my ex-girlfriend is all it took for me to convince myself I could never get stopped for drinking while driving down the interstate if the cruise control was set to the speed limit. I was half lit by the time I drove up to my old apartment. It was the perfect setting for an argument early that afternoon.

The weekend was so tiring. I spent over twenty-four hours on the road from Friday morning to Sunday evening. Even so, I still found time to drink and get to know a woman. It was time for a break and I was heading back offshore Tuesday anyways. I'd look for a new place to live while offshore. Where would I lay my head tonight? Oh, my parents were going to give me a place to stay for a night so we treated it like I was going just to visit. They knew only the basics about what was happening. I didn't want to tell them too much. It was okay, too. Questions lingering in the air weren't asked as they were so happy to see me.

Once I got back to the rig, I had plenty of time to think with a clear mind. I mentioned very little details to my coworkers at first, however I soon learned about the family aspect of working offshore. People working on offshore rigs soon become family. We spend more time together out there on the water than we do with our families. It's a sad truth and testament to the increased salaries offshore workers earn.

So, about that new family… I found emotional refuge in a couple of coworkers. They were inadvertent supervisors, actually. Somewhere, I heard a phrase that stuck with me. "Surround yourself with people better than yourself. Surround yourself with people you see yourself being like one day." It didn't take long for me to pick these supervisors out on the rig and begin spending time with them. See, I wouldn't give people the time of day while home drinking. They didn't matter to me. They were an obligation, not an opportunity.

Okay back to these offshore folks. I worked with a great bunch of people who quickly offered safe alternatives to dwelling in my sorrows. Truth be told, I loved that girl. I drove myself crazy over her. They helped me change my obsession to working out in the gym and other activities available to us on the rig. I quickly formed a relationship with the baker. She was an attractive lady and often brought me treats straight out of the oven. Our relationship stayed professional, but she gave me some emotional support I can't quite understand. I needed it, I just don't understand it.

Shit, I went off track again. A few guys on the rig would spend time in the gym. I joined in and it soon became my offshore obsession. No, I'm not moving forward too fast. This all did happen in one hitch (a single work shift offshore). I spent nearly a month out there. My sorrows, troubles, loneliness, depression, and all other emotions were kept at bay. They were left somewhere between the shore and the rig. It also helped to speak with people that only took my side. They didn't know my ex. They didn't know my personal life. They only knew the straight laced, clean cut guy that worked on the rig with them. I used them to prop myself up and create a better person.

Once I got off the rig for my first hitch home as a single guy, it was time to move. Of course, there wasn't much moving involved. I left her everything we had. So! Papers were signed and keys were put in my hand. I walked in the place for a moment to drop off my clothes, and then I headed to the furniture store. I bought a bed and a couple other pieces of furniture to get by for a while. Ha, a while. I wasn't concerned about purchasing furniture while there wasn't a woman in my life pushing me to spend money on life comforts. I got my essentials as quick as I could and moved on to socializing.

My next hitch offshore included more of the same, but it started a trend. I got out there and quickly began spending my off time in the gym. I'd spend two hours in the gym a day. It was therapeutic in its own right, but it changed me on several levels. I lost weight quick! (Okay, now I'll go over a few months.) I lost about ten pounds my first hitch and changes were happening. Social media was getting big at the same time. I started posting pictures of the progress I was so proud of so people would take notice. Social media was a good outlet since I was stuck on an oil rig somewhere out in the sea. Women started taking notice to me!

I got to a point where it was standard to meet women through social media and break the ice while I was offshore. We would sometimes talk on the phone while I was still on the rig. Other times, I would just see them when I got back on land. The ice breaker time was great for me though. They got to know me, the real me, while I was offshore and sober. I'd get home and go out with them to get drunk and get laid. It was okay that I got drunk because they already felt like we knew each other. Yeah, they also had no idea about my drinking habits. It was good times!

I was on top of the world! I was making decent money offshore and spending it on good times while back home. I felt like a big shot as I bought new clothes and enjoyed going out at night. I'd dress in a sport coat every night I went out. People would see a well-dressed man sipping brandy on ice. I thought I was the epitome of what every woman wanted and every man envied. Ha! Push aside the drinking to oblivion every time I was out on the town. I'd even drink before a date so I didn't look bad when I only had one or two glasses of wine with my meal. I couldn't function without the gym offshore. I couldn't function without alcohol on land.

My first adverse effect of my new lifestyle came within a few months. I went on a date and it didn't go well. She was in to me, but I wasn't feeling her. We had dinner and then went out to a local bar afterwards. I had the standard glass of wine with a nice dinner and then took her out to one of our hangouts. We knew each other from recent endeavors so we both had friends at this place. I got us a drink while we mingled with others and I still don't know what triggered me, but I had enough. She wanted another at some point soon. I went to the bar to get her a drink and didn't get myself one. She gave me a hard time about not getting myself a drink as well. I was just worried about driving home. I had been drinking all day! Of course, we couldn't have that conversation, though. No one knew about my endeavors earlier that day. They probably wouldn't believe it if I told them the truth.

There wasn't an argument. I simply told her I had to go home, but that was not my intended destination. There was another popular spot friends of mine liked to hang out and I decided to go there instead. I drove to that bar with a somewhat straight mind. I was pissed about the date and needed to release frustration. She was a good girl and wanted to date. I wanted to get in her pants. I think that was the whole deal. Anyways, I turned right instead of left and found myself at another bar. I told myself I was just going for a few minutes. Ha, I also told myself I was going home. A few minutes turned in to a few hours. I also told myself I wasn't going to drink. How could I turn down drinks with friends though? We had fun and then it was time to go home. I don't remember the details of the ride home, before I was stopped by the police.

I denied drinking throughout the whole process and questioned why he even stopped me. He called others to come over with the "DUI expert team". I was civil while speaking to them and they even told me I passed the field sobriety test. They told me that while on the way to the police station. When they questioned me, I referred to my entire night during the date. I didn't mention anything before or after.

Okay so after refusing to breathalyzer tests and further sobriety tests in the station, I was sitting in the jail waiting to be booked. I called and got in touch with a bail bondsman. Without seeing even as much as a holding cell, I was in a taxi back to my truck. The police let me speak with workers at the gas station parking lot and they agreed to let me keep it parked there for twenty-four hours. I didn't need that long. I was pulled over around three in the morning and back in my truck four hours later. "Time to get home and get some sleep!" Oh, first thing first though. I went to the DMV and got a new license before the paperwork went through. *They arrested a suspect for drunk driving and let him go only four hours later, knowing he was going back to his truck to drive home.* Yeah, I took a nap and started the process all over again. Of course, I had to go back to the same bar that night and tell everyone how it went down. I repeated the exact behavior.

Behaviors of the same continued for months. I'd be the perfect employee and someone people looked to for advice while on the rig. I'd be a drunk, inconsiderate asshole while on days off. Somehow, I even convinced myself that was what women were looking for since I rarely found myself lonely. I still felt as though I was on top of the world. The high of feeling like I got off from a charge and having women hit on me every night was exhilarating. It was my reality; the truth didn't matter.

Things seemed normal to me as I continued this behavior. I'd successfully sober up to go to work and excel at my job. I'd come home and trade the success for alcohol. I'd meet women online while offshore and get to know them good enough to break the ice. I'd seal the deal when I got off the rig. I even got off on taken women. There was something about me. They loved me. A couple of married women would regularly call me late at night and ask to come over. I would never mess with any women I knew was married or taken! Well, not sober. We wouldn't talk and I would never initiate conversation. They regularly had moments late at night while out drinking with their girlfriends and I was simultaneously drunk enough to get off on them coming over. I remember feeling ashamed of these actions while sober and bragging about the relationships when out drinking with the guys. These relationships also finished killing any chances of my developing trust in a woman.

I was slowly killing myself. Symptoms of withdrawals started showing up every time I got to work. I still remember one of the old guys from the crew openly complaining about smells in the bathroom. I figure it was an ulcer of some sort, but there was definitely old blood in my stool. The first time it happened scared me pretty bad, but it was soon routine. I'd go through phases. Time at home was planned around alcohol. The interesting part is I would forget what it did to me over the days offshore. Once the process was started the day I got home, I couldn't stop. I couldn't let myself go through the pain of withdrawals until absolutely necessary. So, it was a controlled chaos through my days at home as I drank enough to feel okay while attempting to perform normal activities. I was still working out on the rig and at home. There was a nice gym at my apartment and I used it daily. The accountability of holding myself to a workout regimen kept me from drinking first thing in the morning. I'd have a light breakfast and pre-workout drink instead. Lunch would include my first drinks.

This time period, experiencing withdrawals, was when I first researched the adverse health effects. Signs and symptoms of alcohol withdrawals were clear and present. They presented themselves while I was home and tried to stop drinking for a few days. They were intensified during my first couple of days offshore. I need to stress that I am talking about withdrawals, not a hangover. There are significant differences to these health effects.

God was looking out for me as I was looking for something to hold me to more accountability while at home. I needed something to keep me busy. Just as I couldn't seem to figure out what was going to be my saving grace, my phone rang. A local friend, young aspiring welder that used to spend time at my shop learning the processes, was on the other end of the line. He had been working at a new hot rod shop in town. The owner of the shop was looking for a good suspension and fabrication guy. He wanted to meet me for an interview.

I started work at that shop the next day. I, in my mind, took over as shop manager and fabricator. The owner let me make some decisions on builds and soon I would be letting him know when I could make it to work and when I wouldn't be there. It was good and bad at the same time. The work made me keep from drinking too much and I needed that every day.

My days working there sober would soon end. I didn't have the right mind set and the shop was small enough where no drug or alcohol tests were ever given. It was nothing like the accountability of working for a big oil company. The owner picked up beer in the afternoons when we worked late. Having something to drink at work helped keep me content when I stayed past five in the afternoon. The progression in this routine started. I would stop drinking while I felt like I could still drive home, then leave to get home. I always had a bottle of the strong stuff waiting for me. This part is where I started drinking way too much at night. I'd wake up feeling horrible and had the shakes most of the time. Sometimes, I was still drunk from the night before. Times started calling for morning drinks of alcohol to stop my shaking. I felt it was necessary because my job there was to build parts and weld. I needed steady hands! Shit, I was also sneaking drinks for lunch when my morning buzz would wear off. The endless cycle was beginning once again as my attempt to keep myself busy to keep myself sober failed. I was doing all of this and still going out at night with women to fill my needs of companionship.

This was the year I met one of the most interesting women of my life. I was talking to a girl while offshore and things were looking good. (This isn't the girl, but let me lead in to it.) Okay, so the one I was talking to offshore met up with me the first day I got home from the rig. She and I went out the first couple of nights and the sex was okay, too. I was planning to continue seeing her. That's when something interesting happened. We had a crazy Thursday night partying. We finished drinking at a bar right by my place, thinking we wouldn't get in trouble driving home. This is almost the point where I met my newest obsession. Upon waking up the next morning, I started doing a morning after check of my wallet. My credit card was missing! Only logical explanation was that I left it at my last bar.

The girl of the week and I dressed to get some lunch. I was planning to take her home to get clothes after stopping for my card and picking up food. The first stop changed everything. I parked at the bar and told her I'd just run in to see if they had my card. She agreed to stay in the truck. I walked in the place and up to the bar, only to lay my eyes on the most beautiful blonde. "Hey boo, I think I left my credit card here last night." "You must have had a good night! I was about to take it shopping this afternoon. I need a nice dress." "How about I close this tab over here so I don't get in trouble and I'll take you shopping later. You just have to model the clothes for me." She gave my card back to me with her name and number written on the receipt. I walked out the place looking down at the receipt with a grin on my face. As I put the paper in my pocket and opened the truck door, the girl sitting in the passenger seat asked about my smile. I was so consumed by the interaction with the blonde, I forgot she was in my truck! "Oh, I'm just happy the card was here and I got it back without any problems." I lied my ass off and brought her home, never to call her again.

A few text messages that afternoon led me back to the bar where my new lady was working. She would get off in the evening so we could hang out after. We did just that on a swing located on the front porch of the establishment. It was amazing how well we connected.

It was also amazing how quick I'd screw that up. She was a bartender and I was visiting her constantly. She wouldn't let me buy drinks and loved me hanging out while she worked. My alcoholism would soon run rampant in the relationship. Every aspect of every date involved alcohol. I couldn't control myself in that environment. I remember so little of our last date night. We went out to enjoy some live music. The event was in the early evening and it was a beautiful day. We started off to a good time, but I had been drinking all day. The only other part of the night I remember was stumbling around and trying to get in my truck. I fought with the keys, pressing the remote unlock and jamming the key into the door. I did that for what seemed like hours. Next thing I remember, I woke up laying in the grass near my truck. I must have been passed out a while because I was able to gather myself and realize it wasn't my truck. "Oh, shit. I have to get out of here. Now!" It was a few blocks before I realized exactly where I was. I was only a mile or so from my place so I walked home. It was somewhere around three in the morning.

Waking up the next day was a frantic experience. I was in panic mode for the first moments, then calmed myself. "Time to put on some workout clothes and take a walk." I got dressed and started the mission to find my vehicle. It took me hours to find my truck and once I did, I spent about an hour sitting in the truck regretting the entire previous day. A good lunch followed this time and a stiff drink helped me cope with what I did the day before. Again, I would repeat the same behavior that caused me the pain and sorrow in the first place.

Opportunity of a Lifetime

Wonderful things once again came my way. Towards the end of that year, I received a call from a recent client. He was a drilling supervisor for a major oil company and he wanted to hire me as a site manager trainee. I was on the way home from a work boat job when this call came about so it sounded that much sweeter. My shot at my dream job would soon come!

Life was finally coming together for me, or so it seemed. I was in a new relationship with a gorgeous little brunette with a fiery attitude. She was a perfect complement to my shyness. I was away from home most of the time but she texted me constantly while I was working. She was always ready to go when I got home. She would stay with me every night I wanted her. I thought I had the best relationship.

Of course, nothing is perfect though. We both hid things from each other. I don't know everything she kept from me, but something was peculiar about her story of having a car in a body shop for months. She claimed to have been in an accident before we met and she had to get her car worked on extensively. I believed her as I had no reason not to trust her. I had bought a second truck before we met. Why? I had to put an interlock device in my vehicle due to my previous DUI. I couldn't deal with that all the time. I couldn't take a woman out on a date with that in my truck. Although it was a legal requirement I have the device in my vehicle, I made the decision to purchase another since I was making plenty of money.

Okay so now that I explained our secrets, or my secrets, I can continue. I was making a lot of money at my current job and the phone call I previously mentioned brought the opportunity to make more. First, I would have to take a pay cut while training. All of that was good with me since my mind craved the power of being a boss on a drilling rig. The hiring process took about three months. I would drive to Houston regularly for interviews and pre-employment evaluations. Some of these interviews called for me to leave in the middle of the night so I could get there early the next morning. I would then handle business in the office and get back in the truck to drive hours back to Louisiana. My drive and motivation was like no other. I always worked to get what I wanted. I was also working through my chemical addiction to alcohol.

The results of one pre-employment physical still remain fresh in my mind. The doctor's office called me and told me I was healthy with only one concern. I had elevated protein levels in my urine. They explained to me how I was a young man in my twenties and I should be fine, but it would be wise to keep checking these levels. I already knew what was going on, though. I had been researching my signs and symptoms! Remember? Long term, chronic effects of excessive alcohol consumption caused excess proteins in the kidneys. It also caused the hypertension, fluctuation of bodily fluids, and many other things I knew weren't right with my body.

So, I was eventually hired on with this company. Euphoria set in immediately. I was drunk out of my mind the night before leaving for Houston. It started as a party and ended with my girlfriend and myself having a private party at home. I don't think she really cared about my chance to become a drilling manager. She just always wanted to party. I was happy to have a sexy little female partying with me. Her willingness to go home and take me to bed was an added bonus.

Anyways, I left home late the next afternoon. I used my new truck to get her home that morning. I then proceeded to finish packing and load up my old truck. The new one was good for local driving and stuff like that, but I wouldn't risk driving it for work since it didn't have the interlock. A problem was introduced to me on this day. I blew in the thing around two that afternoon and my blood alcohol level was still above the safe level for it to allow me to start the truck. This would be one of the first times the interlock would haunt me after nights of drinking.

I finally started the truck a couple of hours or so later that afternoon. I got to my hotel at a decent hour, early enough to have dinner and a couple of drinks before getting to bed. I missed the first social event of my new group that night, though. The company hired me as part of a group that was put together as the best new hires. We were supposed to be the pride and future of the company. It was something special for my superiors and I started my career there by missing the first event planned for me. I felt bad while I sat at the bar, eating my food. The drinks made me able to deal with everything while sitting alone that night.

Monday morning came quick and I was ready for it. The few drinks I had at the hotel bar the night before was nothing compared to my usual. My morning was going to be a great one, no matter what.

We all started walking in to the office lobby around the same time that morning. Everyone was early. I hadn't met any of the other new hires, but it was obvious who they were. I walked in and began introducing myself after a minute of scouting the group. An imaginative story of my travel day on Sunday and how delays kept me from making the group dinner was told more times than I care to mention.

Finally, a lady from human resources emerged from atop the lobby escalator. She walked up and introduced herself while explaining what we would be doing that morning. After following her up to what seemed to be a grand conference room, we began our onboarding process. The usual legal stuff and training materials were covered. We continued this process for the rest of the week. It was mostly boring material, but the excitement of being in this position kept us all going. We were also issued laptop computers, smart phones, and company credit cards. It seemed like a dream.

I was still talking with my girlfriend every day, but not nearly as much as on my previous job. I had so much socializing going on with this one. I was put in a hotel with all expenses paid. The bosses even told us we could put a couple alcoholic beverages on the company card in the evenings. We were encouraged to go out together for dinner and drinks. They called it "Team Building". This term always made me laugh when it was mentioned.

Multiple large companies used "Team Building" as code for drinking on the company's dime. I have been a part of this more times than I can remember.

So, with all of this going on, I didn't talk to her much. Our relationship was still fine. We just made up for lost time while I was home. Meanwhile in Texas, I was acting like a single man after working hours. The Monday through Friday day job was a whole new experience for most of us in the group. We even had some women in the group that spent time drinking with us at night. The professional manners between us no longer existed after hours. Oh, and after a few drinks!

Our training took us all over the surrounding areas of Houston, Texas. We always had a new place to try for a good meal or a good time. We all started keeping alcohol in our rooms because it was cheaper and easier to conceal. We got paranoid about buying even a single drink on the company credit card. As the weeks passed, we went through several different classes on operations we were expected to manage. I was one of few that had real world experience on these operations and quickly came to be popular. The popularity was kept in check by my excessive drinking. I'd put down almost a fifth of rum after work each day. There was no regard for what condition I'd be in the morning. Everyone was doing it! Yeah, sure I thought everyone was on my level. A few of us were drinking heavy every day. The rest of the group members were all model employees.

I had nights where a couple of the women from the group came to my room. We had all been "Team Building" earlier so I had no self-control. I had a girlfriend at home, sure. She would never find out. I guess they felt the same about their significant others. Most of the group members were married. I met their spouses at one point on another. The nights I mention were never talked about. We all had so much to lose if anyone would know of our endeavors.

I had a very interesting weekend a few months in the job. The company put us in a resort hotel for a weekend and planned a leadership event a few miles away. The resort was located on a beautiful lake with multiple bars and restaurants on location. I was determined to enjoy the facility despite our vigorous work schedule. Friday afternoon and evening involved some swimming and drinks at the bar. There weren't many other women there and I got bored so it was an early night. Saturday morning came with a wonderful breakfast and gourmet coffee while waiting on valet to fetch my rental car. The luxury of this place was impressive.

I thought about how I was going to enjoy the resort that night while driving to our day events. It was a hot, boring day as I was side tracked and uninterested. "If I can't be home with my girl this weekend, I'll be damned if I don't have some fun." And of course, we didn't finish until around seven that night. I couldn't get back to my room fast enough!

My night started sometime around ten o'clock. I walked in to the piano bar after having a couple of drinks in my room while freshening up. The bar maid was the best-looking woman in the place. I knew I wouldn't last long but I was hungry and thirsty. This place had appetizers to go with drinks. Thirty minutes later, I walked over to the night club area. The crowd was thin at first with a few of my coworkers hanging out near the bar. I visited with them until a flood of people came in to the place. A private party of some sort ended and they all showed up to party. "YES!" That was exactly the type of thing I was looking for at the moment. I was turned on at the opportunity to meet new people and hook up with someone random. A few women stayed at the club after their boyfriends, husbands, whoever they were went to bed. The rest of my group had already gone to bed, too. We had the closing events for the leadership thing starting at eight Sunday morning. I didn't care. I was on a mission. And, these women took a special liking to me. They must have been as drunk as I was because we had the most fun I can't remember. One hooked up with me after a little while of flirting. Well, we fooled around out by the lake. We were close to going all the way when I guess she realized what she was doing. "Now, it's time for bed!" It was for the better anyways. Something hit me as I neared the elevator while heading to my room. I partially pissed my pants while waiting for that elevator. There was a fake tree in the elevator foyer that got a good soaking by me as I managed to get half of it on myself. The elevator door opened to show an empty space and no one in the lobby saw what happened. If they did, they didn't confront me. I didn't cross paths with a single person as I made my way to my room. God was trying to tell me something. He wanted to make a statement of disapproval and make me realize what I was doing before I got in trouble.

I kicked the urine soaked pants off and flopped to my bed around four in the morning, only to wake up at eight thirty in a panic. I was still drunk from my night and already late for work. If that wasn't enough, I couldn't simply rush out the hotel. I had to pack up my bag and check out before leaving. It was around ten that morning when I pulled up to the work event and my boss two levels up greeted me with a stern attitude. He took my absence that morning personally. He single handedly planned this weekend for our group and took pride in spoiling us. I took advantage of the situation with a spiteful attitude. Funny thing is he gave me a lecture and a simple, verbal warning. He explained his expectations and personal recommendations for me. In his eyes, I was supposed to become the leader of my group and excel beyond everyone else. We then made our way over to the lounge area and served ourselves lunch. He kept me close and not another word about my absence was spoken by management. I'm sure my coworkers had their own views on my actions.

Why wasn't I humbled by the grace and forgiveness of my boss? Why didn't I see what God was trying to tell me in the hotel that drunken night? I was spared. I was pardoned of inexcusable behavior. I quickly felt like I could get away with anything. My girlfriend even decided to come and visit me that following week. She would stay with me and socialize with the group after work. No one told her about what I had been doing a state away from her. The women that visited me during the night wouldn't say anything. I knew that because they would have their own consequences if we were exposed. There were guys with us that didn't like me, though. Why didn't they tell her about my excavations? All of this enabled me to get worse with everything I did around work.

It only took a few short months for both my relationship and my career to crumble. My boss had a meeting with me one day to voice his concerns on after work activities. He was hearing about what I was doing and the amount of alcohol I was consuming each night. I started isolating myself as much as possible. The bottle in my hotel room was my only friend. Each time we would move locations, I'd run searches on the internet to scout liquor stores. I would plan routes from airports or work events to pass by one and pick up some whiskey or rum. Most cases involved a store far out of the way. Convenience was not a concern as I wanted to make sure no one from work witnessed me at such a place.

Okay, back to the meeting. He had a good talk with me to voice his concerns. He also explained the conversation was going to be considered as a formal, verbal warning. It was also to be considered as an offer to reach out for assistance through the employee wellness program. I didn't have a problem though. I was simply living "the life" as we travelled and partied around work. I drove back to my hotel after barely saying a word to that man who cared about me. I still wasn't ready to admit I was a broken person from alcohol consumption. *I need to drink socially to be accepted.* It was a long drive and I was an emotional wreck.

I got back to the hotel to see a group of coworkers hanging out in the lobby sipping some beer. They waved the normal, casual wave. It was a gesture to be nice, but not so nice as to invite me along. That was fine with me. I made my way to the elevator and received a nice surprise as the doors opened. One of the women I had been close to invited me to dinner. She told me the rest were going to a nearby club and she didn't want to go out late. I told her it would be a nice evening to tell her about what I had been through that day. We did just that. We had a nice meal at a nearby restaurant and enjoyed a couple beers. After only two beers, we went back to the hotel. A casual and somewhat professional evening was spent and we went our separate ways. As I walked in to my room alone, I spotted a half gallon of whiskey from the day before. It was still full. I was always buying extra so I didn't have to make so many trips to the liquor store. Now, I told myself I was going to straighten up after the meeting that afternoon. Problem was, I had enough alcohol in my system from those two beers to completely throw caution in the wind. I drank nearly half that bottle sitting in my room that night. I ran out of ice and soft drinks to mix. No problem, I drank straight from the bottle. After passing out around one in the morning, I woke up later than I should have to be ready for work. We were training at a facility a few miles away. "Okay, I have fifteen minutes to get my shit together and I'll sneak in ten minutes late." I had my plan set in my mind. Well… While speeding down a country highway, I got pulled over by a county Sherriff. He questioned me and allowed me to tell my story after reviewing my paperwork for the car. I presented a very convincing story including many excuses for speeding. First a foremost, I wasn't from Texas and it was my first time in the area. The following excuses were about being late for work, driving a rental I wasn't used to driving, and keeping up with the flow of traffic. That last one should have gotten me. No cars were around! He let me off with the request I slow down. He even explained the speed limits in the areas I would be travelling to work that morning!

I pulled in the driveway to the business where we were training thirty minutes late. Two of my immediate supervisors were sitting in a car out front. They immediately stopped me and confronted me on my tardiness. I don't remember exact details from our conversation, but I ended up in the back seat of their car. They were taking me for a random drug and alcohol screening. I knew I drank a lot the night before, but I didn't know where my blood alcohol content would be. I was soon to find out. They seemed frantic and motivated to catch me as they placed call after call. Supervisors, human resources, clinics, and others were all on the other end of conversations about the situation. We finally pulled up to a clinic around ten thirty. It was after eleven in the morning before I was brought back for my screening. I remember urinating in a cup while hearing one of the supervisors fussing in the next room. "I don't care about urinalysis! I need him to take a breathalyzer now! We have already wasted enough time. Get him to the machine before I really get pissed!" He was so anxious to get me. His anxiousness wasn't needed though. I blew about twice the legal limit around eleven thirty that morning. My heart dropped when I saw the results ticket. I didn't drink that morning, so it was all residual from the night before. My last drink was consumed almost twelve hours before I took that test.

A couple of phone calls between the supervisors and our boss that met with the day before put us on the way back to the hotel. I was told to get to my room and pack up for travel the next day. I managed to get things ready while drinking the rest of the half gallon still in my room. (How does a person still turn to the poison for consolation on the troubles brought about from that very poison?) It was time to turn in my computer, phone, and company credit card that afternoon. I went to my supervisor's hotel room to return the devices after drinking and packing for a couple of hours. I'm sure, for him, it was confirmation of my character. I don't remember what he told me, but he did hand me a travel itinerary for the next day. I read over it back in my room as I finished that bottle and sobbed. My career was over.

What about that relationship I talked about so much? Yeah, that was done too. The difference with that was she wouldn't go away. I broke up with her after a drunken escapade. We went for a day long motorcycle ride one beautiful Saturday about a month before I lost my job. It was such a great day. When we got within a couple miles of home, I stopped over at a bar for a beer. That turned in to her getting drunk. I held back since I was on my bike. That's the only reason I wasn't cutting up with her. Anyways, she got to the point where I was scared she would fall off the motorcycle, so I asked a couple friends of ours to watch her while I went home to get my truck. She flipped while I was gone. She went from a happy, crazy girl to complete asshole when she realized I left her at the bar. I pulled up in my truck and she was ready to fight. We calmed her down enough to change the subject and then she wanted to eat. "Sure babe!"

I was happy to put some food in her stomach and take her home to bed. Things got interesting at this point.

She started getting loud and made a scene in the restaurant. What started this? Of course, it was my fault. She wanted to sit in my lap and start making out at our table, located in the main dining area. There was a family with a table full of kids next to us! I left our food as I was able to get her outside. I put her in the truck and proceeded to get in the driver's side. As I was putting the truck in reverse, she punched me on the right temple with the force of a man. Every fiber of my body was on fire as I threw the truck in park, walked around the passenger side, and pulled her out with her belongings. I got back in my truck and left, making as though I went home. Unable to leave her in that condition, I turned around and parked in a parking lot across the street where she didn't know I was located. I called her family and explained the situation as I kept a watch to make sure she was okay. They picked her up and I never saw her again.

Sounds cut and dry since I never saw her after that day. Not. My phone rang constantly from text messages and calls. She claimed to be pregnant for three months following that day. Try taking control of your alcoholism during that kind of mind fuckery going on every day. And like I said, I was trying to take control of my drinking while unable to admit I was an alcoholic. I didn't want to quit, I wanted to control it.

The Rebound

In the midst of my personal problems, I returned to my parent's home without a job. I told them just enough information about my termination to get them off my back. The phone calls and messages from the ex-girlfriend would continue even after I was home, but a new prospect had my attention. An easy opportunity for a new relationship came around and I took advantage. I found consolation in a young mother going through a divorce. She was beautiful and mistreated. With everything she had been through, she tried to help me deal with my ex and get over everything going on in my life. We snuck around for a while before exposing our relationship. Sure enough, I would then have several close encounters with her ex-husband. This was a relationship I knew to be a rebound for her and something I should have never done. I couldn't offer anything to her. My drinking was getting worse. Her young son needed a man to look up to as a father figure. I couldn't get past being a selfish drunk. She even looked beyond several occasions where I drank to oblivion. She didn't deserve me and I definitely didn't deserve her.

So, I got bored in the stagnation of unemployment. I was at a bar one afternoon when I decided to make the call. Stepping outside with a whiskey drink in my hand, I dialed my old boss from a year before. He was so excited to hear from me! "Do you want to start tomorrow?" I agreed to begin the process and call a start day the following Monday. The paperwork was sent to me the next morning and... "Oh Shit!" I had to call the office and ask if the day rate was correct. The amount on paper would be equal to three times the largest annual salary I ever made in my life. I signed those papers before they had a chance to change the offer.

I also got a crazy little brunette monkey off my back that week. The ex-girlfriend called me again accusing me of abandoning her as she was carrying my child. Well, I got in touch with the doctor's office she claimed to be going. They never heard of her! So, I called her back and let her know that I was excited to support her and I made an appointment for us to see our baby on a 3D ultrasound. She let me know there was no pregnancy the morning of the appointment.

Life seemed to be getting back to where it was supposed to be heading as I put the ex behind me and had a great job coming up. My current girlfriend was supportive and excited for me as well. This would mark the beginning of the end for us, though.

The position I accepted was to function as a consultant on a drilling rig that wasn't on contract just yet. I was to work in the office for three months before finally getting on the rig. Those three months were interesting to say the least. Two weeks in to the office in Houston, I had a female "friend" visiting me for a couple of days at a time. The nights she wasn't at the hotel with me were spent with my coworker. He and I were having a good time exploring the night scene.

We did this routine for a month or so. It was Houston during the week and weekends were spent at home with the girlfriend. After that first month, they approved me to work in the New Orleans office. It was on! I didn't have a boss at this place and I used it to my advantage. Let's be clear, I completed all my work ahead of schedule and exceeded expectations. Now, the thing is I made my own hours. I got to the office when I wanted and left early if I completed assignments. During all of this, I spent plenty of time in the French Quarter and on Bourbon Street. It was both Heaven and Hell for me in my alcoholic state.

I soon found myself a girlfriend there as well and she was only after the one thing I was interested in too. She would show up in the evenings and do our thing.

Sometimes, we would go out. Sometimes we wouldn't. I remember sitting at the bar in my hotel the first night she got there and told me she just wanted to go to bed. She grabbed my hand and led me to the elevators. My head was spinning as I wondered if this could be real. I tell you, we walked in my room and she got her way with me. When we were done, she made us each a drink and we visited. It was still early when she told me she had work the next day and decided to leave. "You mean to tell me this girl just wants sex from me! I don't have to waste time dating and spending money going out. Plus, she leaves after so there aren't any awkward moments the next morning." I knew I was going to be doing as much work as possible out of the New Orleans office.

Meanwhile, my girlfriend back at home saw me when I made it in town and came meet me in New Orleans on a couple of occasions. The two women never interfered with each other. No calls or texts at awkward moments. No running into or seeing each other by accident. It was a lucky time for me. Lucky for my drinking, too. I was late for work only once that whole time. It was a Friday and everyone in my department had off as they worked every other Friday. I went out the night before and got blackout drunk. It was so bad I don't know how I made it back to the hotel.

Just after the holidays, I was in New Orleans leading a training session for rig personnel. My coworker and I were tasked with teaching compliance and expectations to every person from every company stepping foot on our drilling rig. I was excited, nervous, anxious, confident, scared, you name it. My partner and I had a few too many drinks meeting the crew and settling our nerves during "Team Building" events the night before the first day of the three-day event. The first day was hosted by the operations team so we weren't worried about being fresh in the morning. And we weren't, either. We joked about having a drink with breakfast to feel better, but neither of us did. We were too worried about our jobs. All of management attended these sessions.

The first day was a long one listening to all the presenters do their part. My partner and I discussed how we could manage things better and make the next two days more enjoyable for the crew members. We decided to both take it easy on the drinks and get to bed by ten o'clock that night and the next. We also decided to tag team the presentations with breaks in between each session. We would breeze through the tedious sections and spend more time on the parts pertaining directly to the rig crews. We had a plan!

It was all business for the two of us those days. We gave an excellent presentation with good reviews from crew members and management too. With the end of the training session marking a successful milestone for both of us, it was time to celebrate. We wanted to get out of the hotel and decided to find a sports bar for the afternoon. I volunteered to drive and wait to drink once we made it back to our hotel that evening. I felt good doing it and my partner was all about it. He was ready to drink some beer. I think I just knew if I started that early, it would be very bad. I had no idea that night would mark the beginning of the greatest change of my life.

It was a guy's afternoon spent unwinding from work and flirting with women. We had a good time visiting with the waitresses at the sports bar, and then I drove us back to the hotel. My partner drank almost a dozen beers while I had unsweet tea and enjoyed my meal. It was a good time for me without drinking any alcohol. I think my mind let me enjoy it because I knew I'd catch up once we made it back. The alcoholic mind is something of an enigma.

We walked in to an empty bar and I felt comfortable. All of our crew members from the rig left the hotel and I could finally cut loose. The bartender was a lovely lady many years older than me, but good company for two guys kicking back drinking. The bar gained a few more occupants as the day turned to night. I was quickly catching up to my buddy's buzz as I drank scotch on ice. A lady sat next to me at one point and I had an easy opportunity to flirt. The afternoon filled with good times and my partner pulling women my way had me wishing for a woman's company in bed. This particular one was eating up everything I told her. She asked me about work, about my interests, my tattoos. She seemed so intrigued with everything I said to her.

Then! Something happened. A woman in a baseball cap across the bar called bullshit on something I said. "Who the fuck are you?" I said her way as I tried to continue with my mission. She swiftly replied. "I know exactly who you are. I just had to sit and listen to you speak for hours over the past days." I did not recognize the woman, but I had a bad feeling as I knew she was a part of the rig crew. Our conversation wasted no time in killing my chances with the lady to my right. She was on to visiting with the next guy. I figured I'd give this one a shot as she seemed to be a bit of a fiery one and I liked that about a woman. (Obviously, given my track record.) We talked for the rest of the night. It seemed like hours, but I really don't remember how long we visited. The scotch kept flowing and prevents my memory from serving me clear thought of the night. I do remember letting her tell me about herself and us seeming to "hit it off". I tried making a move on her in the elevator on the way to our rooms and she shut me down. It was justifiably so. Ha, I couldn't have done anything if she did want to get under the sheets. She gave me her number and said to get in touch the next day if I wanted to see her again.

We couldn't have been up very late that night because I woke up fairly early the next morning. My mind was as cloudy as the rainy New Orleans skies. I remembered the couple of things mentioned already and nothing more. Anyways, I did the morning after checks of my wallet and phone. Everything was in place and I had her number saved. The only problem was I couldn't quite remember exactly what she looked like! I remember being attracted to her. I was impressed and turned on about her stopping my advance in the elevator the night before. She even worked offshore! Could this lady be the one for me?

My partner and I met up in the lobby that morning before going to the office. We had some equipment from our presentations to return before going home. While I got questioned about my time spent with "the girl in the cap", we got a little work done. It was fun letting him give me a hard time about her and my curiosity finally got the best of me. I texted her from the office and surprisingly received a quick response. We exchanged a few messages that morning. I soon found myself sitting in the parking lot of a restaurant somewhere along the interstate as I waited for our lunch date. A problem came to mind as I sat in my truck. I didn't remember what she looked like!

Luckily, she told me what she was driving and I watched her pull up. Then, I walked over to the door of the restaurant and she was wearing the same baseball cap. "Yes! Confirmation!" We had a good time while eating at a little deli and getting to know each other. I honestly don't remember the details of our conversation, but I remember leaving with a good feeling. We left that place headed home to very different places.

We stayed in touch by text message every day. There was the occasional phone call, but that was mostly to set up our first real date. I had to be careful as I was still dating the young lady from home. Since I was home, we were together just about every day over the following week and a half. That was the time I had before leaving to go offshore. I managed to escape to a hotel near the woman I just met by way of a guy's motorcycle trip. A friend of mine lived within a decent drive of her place and I used the coincidence to open a window of opportunity. I got in touch with her and our first real date was planned.

That weekend came quick and I left with the bike. Arriving to the hotel my first night, I had some drinks there and went to bed. The next morning was an early one and I was ready. I unloaded the motorcycle from my little trailer for a long day of riding. Yes, I trailered it. I had to pack things for a couple of nights and bring some good clothes for my date! Get off my back! Ha-ha, moving along. I rode around to the front of my hotel and decided to run up to my room for a last-minute drink. My nerves had me shaking with a ride involving so many lanes of traffic ahead of me. I had to settle down a little bit.

The day was a long but good one on the open road. Two guys riding in the wind, through the hills and in the sunlight. It was something I hadn't done in a while in a place I hadn't even been. We stopped every hour or so to stretch our legs. A nice little sports bar was the perfect spot for lunch with a couple beers. We got close to my temporary home just as it was getting dark.

I walked in the lobby from my ride and couldn't bring myself to pass the hotel bar. I was worn out from the ride and sore from the saddle. The young lady behind the bar was a sweetheart as she served my whiskey drinks over the next thirty minutes. That's all the time I had before I needed to shower and clean up. She was kind enough to fix me two drinks for the walk upstairs. Well, those drinks and less than an hour later, I was a new man sitting in that same bar. The lady behind the bar didn't even recognize me at first so I must have cleaned up well. She kept a full glass in front of me while I waited for the lady of the night to pick me up. Yes, we set our date for her to pick me up from my hotel. I was in her town with a truck, trailer, and motorcycle. She took me to a nice Mexican restaurant that evening. It wasn't over the top, but just enough for us to enjoy each other's company while having margaritas. Dinner went well and she got down with me at my hotel. She would go as far as to keep me company in the quiet hotel bar. It was a nice place with a good atmosphere. I was tired, but hoping she would decide to come up to my room. Nope. She had a couple drinks and was out the door with a quick kiss. I think the night went well.

The Contract

We stayed in touch a little and saw each other again on the drilling rig. I figured things were going better than I first anticipated when she started visiting my office on a daily basis. We were determined to keep our relationship professional and private, especially when it came to anyone on the rig finding out. There were technically no rules against a relationship between two consenting adults working on a rig together. We worked for different companies and did not violate any policies at work. It was, however, frowned upon. So, we kept things as our little secret.

I was still in a relationship with that sweet girl from home, sort of. Our relationship had dwindled down to text messages. As I tried to be a good man, I called her and had a conversation on ending our relationship. We weren't going to make it long term and we both knew it.

With that being said, I kept getting closer to my new lady. She had an attitude that could handle the guys on the rig. I thought that was amazing. She was sweet on me though. Her facial expressions changed, her mannerisms were different, and she took up for me when guys messed with me. It was sweet. This lady got to know the real me over the next few months.

I didn't get much time off during the following three months. The few that I did were spent with my lady. I didn't care if we hadn't had the chance to date more than a few times. We saw each other almost every day and visited every chance we could. Quite honestly, I don't remember the circumstances we first slept together. I think it was at her place after a nice dinner, but it's not clear. My mind was poisoned with alcohol every day on land. It's a damn shame to miss so many memories, but it's what happens to a mind poisoned from alcohol. The first three months were good though. We made the long hitches offshore enjoyable for one another.

I quickly fell for her as I was so comfortable. All my insecurities from previous relationships vanished with this woman. She adjusted her work schedule to match mine so I didn't have to worry about her in bars or cheating on me while I was working. That nullified the ghost of one ex-girlfriend. On top of that, she empathized with me when I spoke of my feeling on the rig. She was also capable of having intelligent conversations about work.

Our relationship changed exponentially that Spring. I forget if she ever got on the back of my motorcycle with me before this particular day. I hope this wasn't her first ride with me. Anyways, she got off the rig a couple of days before me. She went home a state away and returned with her things to spend a few days with me at my place. The last few times we dated were at her place so she was ready to see a new place more in depth. My first night off the rig was spent in the bars. She kept me company as I showed her a few of my local spots. This girl could hold her liquor, too. We killed it that night. I don't know how much I drank because I just spent weeks in sobriety on the rig. All I do know is it was enough to blackout and wake up early the next morning with a splitting headache. I left the house to fill up the motorcycle before our ride and managed to pick up a pint of vodka. I didn't even think about it when I bought it. I returned home to finish detailing the motorcycle and downed the vodka straight while she showered.

By the time she was finished getting dressed, I was inside getting some breakfast ready. We had some food with orange juice and coffee, then strapped on the helmets for our day ride. We took our time going down the first country road as I made sure she was feeling comfortable. She held on tight and I enjoyed feeling her legs squeeze along mine as I accelerated. My last memories of this ride occurred just under three miles from its origin. I attempted to pass a car that was driving slowly on a country road. I had no idea the driver of the vehicle was attempting a left hand turn as I twisted the throttle back as far as it would go. The brakes had no match for the amount of acceleration I just put forth. Witnesses say the skid marks were over fifty feet long. I only remember a split second of slamming brakes and trying to get back to the right side of the road as the vehicle turned left. I hit a small sport utility vehicle directly in the rear axle. Consciousness was lost for me, immediately.

Witnesses tell me that I bounced directly back from the broadside impact. I looked dead. My passenger went over the vehicle and landed on the road several feet beyond it. Luckily, she stood up within seconds and without a scratch. I was put on a spine board by medics and air lifted to the hospital. I woke up some time that afternoon.

I was in a hospital bed and the whole thing felt like a dream. I couldn't move my head as I attempted to look around the room. Slowly, I tried to move my arm to assist my efforts in sitting up. My right arm seemed to lift, but my left wouldn't budge. "Oh shit, I'm restrained to the bed." I started mumbling my thoughts and this alerted the occupants of the room to my consciousness. "Be still.

You're lucky to be alive." "Do you know where you are?" "Do you realize what you've been through today?" All of these statements began filling my ears though I was groggy and my mind clouded. A nurse appeared and began explaining my condition to me. Soon after, a young doctor walked in and stood beside my bed. He asked me a couple of questions about the incident. I don't remember his questions and can only assume he wanted to determine my level of understanding before telling me a few things. He told me to be as still as possible overnight. He said my neck was broken in the C-2 vertebra. "The vertebra is fractured. The bone fragment did not shift and you are very lucky. If the fragment shifts, you will either die or be paralyzed." He continued to tell me that my left arm was broken with a compound spiral fracture. He said he couldn't do surgery until the next morning. With no questions to answer, he left the room.

My family was in the room and began asking me how I was feeling. They were concerned about my wellbeing and upset with me at the same time. It wasn't my first time doing something stupid on the motorcycle they hated so much. It was, however, the worst accident I had ever been in my entire life. I started asking about my girlfriend. I guess she was in the room the entire time, I just couldn't see her. She walked closer to the bed and started talking to me. I couldn't believe she didn't have a scratch, bump, or bruise on her body. She told me how the medics let her ride in the helicopter with me to the hospital. She got checked out and cleared right away. I was so relieved to hear of her good health. I was okay with hurting, even killing myself. I couldn't live with hurting her.

The topic of conversation turned a different direction. She mentioned the medics saying something about a smell of alcohol on me. I don't remember exactly what I said, but it was something about the night before. I told her it must have been residual from our crazy night out. She and everyone else believed me, or so I thought. But, I couldn't help but asking about the police. "Did they give tickets? The police, did they draw blood from me or take any other kinds of samples for analysis?" I told them my concern was from the night before and I was just asking since she mentioned a smell. "No one took any samples or issued any tickets that we know of. Everyone was worried about saving your life." I was somewhat relieved, but still skeptical. They didn't know about what I did that morning before our ride. And I wasn't about to tell them.

I endured a five-hour reconstructive surgery on my arm the next morning. The physicians confirmed the reason behind my lack of movement in my left appendage.

The break severed a main nerve that controlled all movements in my lower arm, hand, and fingers. I felt what it was like to be paralyzed. A week or so of hospital care turned in to home care at my family's house. I needed help performing the simplest life functions.

The next few weeks bared a hardship on all my family members. The very people I hurt by drinking alcohol were taking care of me. The woman I almost killed on the back of my motorcycle was helping me bathe, dress, urinate, defecate, eat, and everything else in between. What is the worst part about all of this? I still wasn't myself! I traded my alcohol for very strong narcotic pain killers. The doctors prescribed all the pain killers I could ingest. I used them too. The first couple of weeks involved legitimate pain, but progression set in just as it always does with someone like me. I was soon doubling up on them to get a buzz on top of getting me through the pain. I was feeling sorry for myself as I was learning how to live with my left arm strapped to my torso. I should have felt sorry for the ones dealing with me.

My poor girlfriend took care of me every day she was off the rig and never missed a day of work. She kept our relationship secret and never wavered. All I can say is, wow. The weeks passed by and I was able to take my neck brace off. The doctor reviewed up to date x-rays showing the fractured C-2 healed. What a miracle of God! I was high from the narcotics the six weeks prior and barely wore my neck brace. I had to reason no understand His mercy. But, I was on my way to healing. The physical therapy for my arm was going well and the nerve was healing. The feeling and motor function of my lower appendage was returning at a rate of one millimeter per day. People from work were even calling to check on me. My boss had to put temporary guys in my place, but requested I work from home to provide support and guidance to the rig. I never missed a paycheck. How many blessings could I get in a lifetime?

My improvements allowed for the return of my independence. I started drinking again just as soon as I got out on my own. There was an additional problem this time, narcotics. I was still taking pain killers! The physicians continued my scripts as long as I wanted them, plus they were cheap. The negative consequences during this time affected my family. They saw the worst of me. I went on a week-long vacation with my girlfriend. My cousin was having a destination wedding and we decided to make the most of it. Together, we visited so many sights and attended events during that week. Some of these places included were bucket list type stuff for me. I barely remember any of it. My memory serves me snap shots of the days leading up to the wedding. I'm told I was a complete asshole to my parents and people around me during a party before the wedding. The only things I remember of that night were getting drinks and sitting at a table watching people as the room seemed to sway back and forth. My girlfriend and I didn't get invited for other social events with my family. Well, I didn't get invited. She didn't go because she opted to take care of me. I don't remember my cousin's wedding at all. I know that I bought a very expensive suit to wear that day and I don't even remember wearing it. What a fucking waste...

The return of that trip served as the end of my days off. I still didn't have full function of my left hand and that wouldn't return for months. I was able to grab things at this point, just couldn't extend my fingers. Management reviewed my condition and decided to allow my return. They sent me to a training event involving rig personnel first, with the schedule showing my flight offshore the following week. I was motivated with this news and sorrowful about hurting my loved ones the prior week. I flushed all the prescription medication left and would never again refill them. Somehow, that was fine with me and at the same time I celebrated my achievement with a drink. Will anyone ever truly understand the alcoholic mind? I doubt it.

The training event was a nice return to reality. My girlfriend was on the rig and I was visiting with crew members who wanted all my attention. I answered so many questions as we drank all afternoon and night while "Team Building". They all wanted to see wounds and picked on me about my left hand. It was actually refreshing to make light of the situation. The event went well.

Back on the rig, I got picked on every day and it was all fun. I spoke with the guys about my injuries and ultimately decided to use them to my advantage. I made a couple of presentations on hand injuries. It worked well since the company was making a push for hand safety and I could make it personal. The following four months or so went well. I worked my ass off while on the rig and drank socially while home with my girlfriend. Life was just the way I figured it should be.

Just as my consciousness was always a drink away, so were the consequences. I was at home drinking and packing for another "Team Building" event one evening when I passed out. I was at home with no plans to leave. My agenda included packing my bag and having dinner at home while drinking whiskey. My girlfriend helped me control my drinking through accountability. She wasn't with me this night, though. I lost consciousness at home on my couch. I woke up in the back of a police car over fifty fucking miles from my home. I had no idea where I was or what I was even doing there! I recognized my truck in the shadows of flashing blue lights. "Oh my God, what happened?"

The police explained that I was stopped for suspected DUI without incident. They took me on a thirty-minute ride to the station. It was some type of temporary building or something like that. I remember sitting there keeping quiet. There was no resistance or provocation from me, but I didn't cooperate. A bondsman took my debit card information a couple of hours later and I was in a taxi headed home. They provided me with the information on my truck so I could pick it up, too. I took care of everything overnight and somehow got back home for a nap around nine o'clock in the morning. I even had a shiny new license. The rest of the day seemed to drag as I knew I had to leave for the work event that afternoon. I had my truck parked in its spot, my license in my wallet, and no one knew what happened. Whoa! It took me the whole drive to New Orleans to figure out if the whole ordeal was reality or a bad dream. My bank account proved it to be true. Still, I couldn't tell my girlfriend for she would definitely leave me. I got to the hotel and started drinking. The consequences would quickly be forgotten, even if it was temporary.

She and I packed all her belongings a month after the DUI. She still had no idea and I was so nervous during the round trip to Texas. My temporary license expired either that day or the next. Either way, I'd have to pull that paperwork if the police stopped us. I wasn't drinking, but wished I could just to calm my nerves. So, hours on hours of travel and packing / unpacking proved to be uneventful. The relief of finishing our moving experience was satisfying for both of us. She had no idea how much of a relief it was for me to get off the roads. Our life together in Louisiana was beginning now that we were sharing an address. Somehow, we even continued to work together offshore. Life was great! We spent every damn waking minute together! And... This would be the point I started sneaking alcohol just as I did in the past relationships. I did it while realizing what I was doing while drinking to cope with what I was doing. You get all that?

She didn't question me so much at these points in time. I could see concern in her eyes every time I looked at her. But we were new to living together and loved each other so much! She loved me, no doubt. She took care of me while I put her though so much over the year of our relationship. I like to think I loved her, but I'm not sure I've ever been capable of love. I didn't want to be without companionship, sex, or alcohol. I needed to feel wanted by someone. Those were my feelings. Please don't ask me the definition of love. It's a mysterious word to an alcoholic.

Angels and Demons

A couple of months after we started living together marked the end of her offshore career. Oh, what happened? I received a message from her while offshore. She asked me to call her as soon as possible because she had something important to discuss. Yes, I know we had the same work schedule but I was never one to turn down work. I always worked over when possible. She answered the phone and something was different in her voice. I could hear so many emotions through my office phone. The last time I worked over left us lonely for each other. We had an amazing date the night I finally got home from the rig and love making was amazingly emotional. The sexy black dress she wore out didn't last five seconds through the door when we got home and no amounts of prior consumed alcohol kept us from becoming one for the rest of the night. I was never careful when it came to making love with this woman. Something felt as though we were just doing what was spiritually right.

I was going to be a father. She took six pregnancy tests before asking me to call her and she was still doubtful as to their accuracy. I comforted her and expressed some excitement in hopes to ease her worries. A local clinic a phone call away congratulated me as a new daddy when I explained our situation. God was sending me an angel to love and protect. But how was I supposed to take on such a task when I was drinking more than ever? I knew I needed to quit and made the decision to do just that! I won't drink, I can't!

Crew change day finally came around and I was headed straight home. I couldn't wait to hold my beautiful girlfriend and tell her about how excited I was for us to have a baby. Half way home, I needed gas and stopped to fill up. I was paying for my fuel and a soft drink when I told the cashier to put a fifth of vodka on my tab as well. I finished the bottle as I pulled in my parking spot at home without a thought about what just happened. She greeted me at the door and I hugged her before putting my bags down. It didn't hit me until I put my things up and sat down on the couch. I woke up hours later, in her arms. This sweet young lady was in a state of frustration and confusion as she held the unconscious body of the man she loved so much.

I got defensive when I woke up. I was mad at myself and confused as to why I did what I did earlier that day. We got in to a little bit of an argument and I made the reoccurring promise of never drinking again. She thought I was intentionally lying to her when I broke these promises, though she will probably never understand the promises were broken to my own soul as well. I made an excuse to leave the house.

Riding around near home, I couldn't seem to gather my thoughts. How was I going to make this up to her? The lasting effects of the alcohol still in my system probably had something to do with that, but it also had something to do with my next actions. I managed to visit with a jeweler I knew and purchased an engagement ring. A proposal with a beautiful ring would most definitely get me out the dog house. I was so happy with my purchase; I stopped to get another drink on the way home. The details of that night elude me, but I'm sure they wouldn't be found in a fairy tale story.

She and I were going to a baseball game two nights later. We both enjoyed watching the sport and my local team was playing a home game. I spent the afternoon in my garage drinking and turning wrenches before getting dressed for the game. During that time, my mom and I spoke on the phone. I told her about the ring and my plans to propose. She invited us to join her and my dad in New Orleans for the weekend for Mardi Gras. She had an idea and mentioned I should propose in the French Quarter. I agreed we would go meet them and might have even agreed to her idea to avoid conflict, though there wouldn't have been any conflict. My wet brain told me to do shit like that all the time because I always endured some type of conflict when I drank around the ones who knew me.

Okay, back to the game. We left in my truck and scenarios were running through my mind. For some reason, I kept hearing the voice of an ex-girlfriend. Remember the one that was engaged when I met her? She always told me that she agreed to the proposal because he did it in front of a crowd with family and friends. I got to a point where I couldn't take the anxiety anymore. We were halfway across the parking lot, walking to the game and I made an excuse to go back to my truck. I asked my girlfriend to wait there and I'd run to the truck and back. She agreed and I hurried back to the side of the truck where she couldn't see me. I grabbed the engagement ring and downed the rest of a whiskey pint that was in my console. The proposal itself is the only thing I remember of the rest of the night.

I sat there drunk and anxious as we watched the ball game. I picked a point where nothing was happening on the field and turned to her with the ring pulled out my pocket. I was simply sitting next to her professing my love and asking her hand in marriage as I presented the ring in a somewhat inconspicuous way. (I didn't want a scene.) She agreed and held on to my arm with teary eyes once I slipped the ring on her finger. We were officially engaged.

I called and told my mom about my proposal during our drive to New Orleans the next day. We got there and all conversations were about the ring, the pregnancy, and plans for a wedding.

The Catholic Church started presenting us with challenges as we looked for a priest to marry us. We decided on a three-month engagement so she wouldn't be showing too much, so that was a challenge. The greatest challenge was to convince a priest we were getting married for love and not just because of pregnancy. We did it with great determination as some priests still voiced great concern. Did they see right through me? Did they see my alcoholism? Did they know motives behind my actions that I couldn't see myself?

All the busy days together spent planning and looking forward to marriage kept me from drinking. It was a win, win situation and I was grateful. I'd still sneak some alcohol daily but not enough to get blackout drunk. It was just getting me by so I could function normally. My girlfriend was getting sick from pregnancy and my life was turning upside down faster than I could comprehend. This is about the time I messed up again. We had another training session for work a few hours away from home. I got to the hotel and the guys were already drinking heavily. "Team Building!" I felt the need to catch up with them. The drive over prevented me from drinking earlier that day and my tolerance was higher than most people. Anyways, I already had a bottle of 100 proof rum stashed in my bag ready to go. I put the fifth to my lips and drank almost half of it in my room before going back to the lobby. The inside of my body was on fire as I rode the elevator down but it was momentary. We were soon piling in a cab headed to our restaurant. A few drinks over there had me feeling drunk enough to agree with joining the group headed to a strip club. I was determined to get things off my mind that night.

The next thing I remember is waking up in my hotel room to a phone call from my fiancé. She was so sick; she was scared and crying frantically. I could only think about getting home to her and be there for her. My next memories of that day are snapshots of an empty rum bottle, sitting in the parking lot of a gas station, and sitting in a police car before going to jail. I don't know if I drank that morning, the bottle was the same one I started the night before. I don't know where the gas station was located, I was lost. The officer stopped me headed down the interstate in another state. These thoughts ran rampant as I lay in my holding cell. I got to the jail just before noon and bailed out before five that afternoon. They let me go and had my truck waiting for me, even though I had a suspended license and DUI charge. I didn't think twice about getting back in my truck and finding my way home. My fiancé and my boss had both been trying to get in touch with me all day. I used her as an excuse to why I wasn't at work and I used work as to why I wasn't home yet.

This event weighed on my conscious for nearly a week before I told my fiancé about everything. This incident triggered things to come up about the last one that she still didn't know about. I confessed everything in tears. I told her about my struggles and intentions to quit drinking while unable to succeed. She needed to know what she in for and who she was marrying. The love in her eyes shined through as she held me and agreed to work through everything together. I still don't know if it was her love or her hope for our child.

Till Death Do Us Part

As the wedding came close, nothing much changed. I was trying and failing to sneak alcohol every day I was home from work. She was dealing with everything on her own while also having to deal with me. The families came together for a rehearsal and dinner the night before our wedding. I had been drinking all day, of course. Her family showed up around lunch time that day and I had already put down a pint of vodka. I then decided to take them for lunch and drinks at a nearby sports bar. The afternoon was more of the same while she was at work and her family went to their hotel room.

The rehearsal went okay but I know people could tell I was drunk. I remember being an asshole to my brother's wife. That's the only thing that stuck in my memory. Dinner that night included many more drinks and tensions between some family members. The alcohol brought out comments from some of her family members and I started having heavy anxiety. I don't even know why I was anxious, probably just the amount of alcohol in my system. I would go on to drink myself to sleep that night, only to wake up early the next morning and leave the house for more alcohol. I had the perfect excuse. Some parts ordered the previous week had just come in and I had to get them installed on my truck. We were leaving in the truck the next day for a fourteen-hour drive. I wasn't waiting for my truck without vodka in an energy drink though. My wedding day was starting off to set the tone for my marriage.

The shop finished and I went back home to my family. The women had already started their day of festivities while the guys hung out. I took my time getting dressed while drinking some vodka I picked up that morning. I keep the rest of my wedding day memories by looking through pictures, rather than personal experience. I struggle to remember taking most of the pictures as I thumb through the albums. I remember a frustrated bride as I instructed a waitress at our reception to keep my glass full of rum. I remember wanting to go out after the reception was over, but my new wife making me go home. I soon fell asleep on her as we lay together that night.

She didn't give me a difficult time the next day and I didn't mention a word about alcohol. We loaded up my truck and left that afternoon to begin our honeymoon. Things were looking up for our future together. The following week was a success story of compromise. We were in the smoky mountains for the first time. It was a special trip for our honeymoon as we experienced the place together. My bride had trails mapped out for each day. We hiked until her pregnant body couldn't go anymore, then we would go to town and I would drink moonshine until I couldn't walk straight. She rewarded my good deeds of each day with alcohol in the evenings. Marriage is about compromise and each getting what we want, right?

The months following were an ongoing struggle. She was dealing with her pregnancy and her alcoholic husband. Maybe it was true love. Maybe it was a woman hoping a man would change. Maybe she married the guy on the rig while getting the drunk at home. Maybe she wanted nothing more than her baby to have a father. Whatever it was, she didn't get what she deserved. The worst part about these months is I knew how bad I was acting and still proved powerless over alcohol. Alcohol controlled my thoughts from the moment I opened my eyes in the morning to the moment I lost consciousness at night. I drank for all my wife's doctor visits. I drank outside the doctor's office the morning I heard my baby's heartbeat for the first time. I drank the morning I saw the ultrasound showing my little girl for the first time. Alcohol had a death grip on me every moment of every damn day. My withdrawals were deathly every trip offshore. I had to isolate myself the day we got to the rig because I couldn't eat or even sign my name due to shakes.

My personal projects I used to love to do were overcome with alcohol. It wasn't enough to have a beer or a drink in satisfaction of achievement. I was drinking first thing in the morning and never could complete anything. I wouldn't follow through with promises to anyone. My pregnant wife had to come and pick me up from people's homes when I would pass out there or they would take my keys to protect me. The end was coming.

Sure enough, I was running errands one morning a week before my daughter's due date. I don't remember drinking that morning, but I drank the day before. That point aside, my body was in bad shape. I bumped a post at a gas station and things escalated quickly. I remember going to jail and speaking with my family the next day. Yeah, this time I spent about twenty-four hours in jail. My parents were at the jailhouse with my wife. They picked me up and I agreed to go to the hospital. I wanted it as much as they did, but I was terrified of missing my daughter's birth. We went to a detox center that agreed to take me on immediately. It was a quick stay as they agreed the best route of treatment for me would be outpatient therapy and I didn't have much of a detoxification process to complete.

My daughter's birth would prove to be the most exhilarating event of my life. I was a week sober when she was born and stayed up for hours on end for her to see the world. The doctor allowed me to assist in her birth and I was the first person to hold her. What a miracle! I, for the first time, was the perfect husband and partner in life a woman could ask for. I continued to be that man through our hospital stay. I was even happy to change my baby's first diaper. Everything was going as it should, finally. My mom came to our place and helped with the baby while I concentrated on being my best and continuing treatment. My wife was the perfect partner in support. She even brought me to treatment and Alcoholics Anonymous meetings while my truck was in the shop. The truck stayed in the shop for a couple of months while being repaired, so her dedication to me was nothing to be taken lightly.

I was the model patient in recovery for months. Then things started changing. I was having problems getting an erection and functioning as I should when trying to make love to my wife. I couldn't understand at first, but then I realized it was the medication my psychiatrist had me taking every day. I researched the side effects and asked a couple guys I trusted. They had been through similar troubles and prescribed similar medication.

My solution was based off their recommendations and my own cognition. I took the medication while offshore and started having a beer daily while home. The medication kept me leveled at work and the beer mellowed me just enough at home while allowing me to please my wife sexually. My self-control proved strong for weeks after ruining almost six months of sobriety. It was three months after graduating from treatment when I took that first sip. Still, I attended my daily AA meeting at seven o'clock in the morning. I used the support to keep my confidence high and my wife thinking I was still doing as I should.

The inevitable finally happened and I would be lying to you if I told you when it occurred. I had an ignition interlock in my truck as part of my consequences, but it didn't take me long to figure the thing out. I'd have to be sober to start the vehicle, and then it would go off ten to fifteen minutes later. After that, it was timed at thirty minute intervals. No problem! I'd go to my meeting in the morning and buy alcohol to drink on the way home. I even mapped out the stores in my mind. I knew which ones to stop for the optimal use of the thirty-minute window. The beer turned to bottles and the bottles gradually got larger.

All my drinking coincided with our life changes. I didn't drink the whole time my wife was on maternity leave and managed to stick to the single beer as long as we were comfortable in our apartment. My wife was soon in a full-blown search for a house. She found one she liked and moved forward with the purchase while I was offshore. My dad helped ensure appropriate inspections were conducted while I was at work. He even got the approvals in order and reviewed things to help protect us. I got home and got busy with closing processes and moving our things. Somehow, I was drinking a fifth of hard liquor every day before I realized it. I stopped going to meetings and fell completely off the wagon. It comes back with a vengeance! I not only went straight back to what I was doing before, but I was now better educated on how to get around getting caught. Well I thought I was better, but my wife was catching me every day again. We went from arguing to looks and pouring out bottles. I started hiding bottles with secondary bottles hidden for when she found the first ones. It was bad, to say the least.

She was offered a position back in Texas around this point in time. Her office had her travelling there most of the time I was offshore anyways. We hadn't finished moving in our house and we made the decision it was best to move once again. I told her I could use the change of scenery and I could find treatment of some sort once we settled.

She found an apartment she liked and papers were signed. All of this seemed to happen so fast! My drinking was curbed once again as I was so busy with everything going on. This was short lived and very temporary. I moved most of our belongings to the apartment but kept enough to sustain me for a night or so in the house. I started spending a night or two at the house when I got off the rig, the middle of my days off at the apartment, then another night or two at the house before flying back out. I used the upkeep of the yard and convenience of it being closer to the heliport as my excuse. I just wanted to drink myself unconscious. That's what I did every day I was at that house. I curbed my drinking while at the apartment with my wife and daughter all the while salivating for a drink. Progression of alcoholism would soon do what it does best. I got beyond only drinking heavily at the house. I was soon showing my worst characteristics at the apartment as well.

Separation Anxiety

This particular Friday started out like most any other days I was at the apartment. I was feeling so depressed and it wouldn't go away that day either. My drinking had gotten to a point where I was researching addiction and recovery places around the Houston area on a daily basis. I wasn't following through with anything though. I waited around the apartment after my wife and daughter left that morning. I waited until I was comfortable any alcohol I drank the day before would be out my system and I wouldn't have any worries when attempting to start my truck. "I'm going to get it right today." I told myself when getting dressed to go out to the store.

That shopping experience started out with the best of intentions. I began picking up my supplies to cook my wife her favorite Cajun meal, seafood gumbo. I was determined for it to be the good night and weekend we needed so desperately. As I was driving out of the grocery store's parking lot, there it was. The liquor store was speaking to me. It was so beautiful nestled in that shopping center across the street. "Man, I don't have anything at the apartment to do but listen to the radio on my phone while cooking this delicious meal. I can get something to drink while I cook and put some country music playing. I'll be alone for the next several hours. I can have a couple drinks and sober up before she gets home!" I walked in that store with the best feeling. I was going to have a great afternoon doing some cooking and still have a nice evening with my wife. "I might even look at some recovery center websites while the gumbo simmers." I said while driving to the apartment.

My afternoon started off according to plan. On arrival to the apartment, I grabbed my groceries and 100 proof fifth of rum from the truck. Once everything was on the kitchen counter, I began laying out my ingredients. It was something I started doing a long time ago and it would make me feel as though I was cooking professionally. I'd even post pictures of everything ready to start going in the pot on social media at times. The positive comments would make me feel so good and of course I'd follow up with pics of my final product. I knew I was just looking for attention though.

So! Bell peppers and onions were chopped up just right and in a bowl. The shrimp were peeled and deveined, mixed in a bowl with the rest of the seafood ingredients with seasoning. It was time to turn the stove top on and get to my favorite part, cooking and drinking. That bottle opened easily and the rum poured in my tumbler with a rhythmic flow. The soda made a crisp noise when the bottle popped open. The two mixed perfectly as I couldn't wait for a taste. I drank nearly half of that drink by the time I had to think about checking on my water. I was so excited! I finished the first drink and made another to sip while cooking down my roux. Once my gravy reached the correct color and consistency, it was time to start putting my ingredients in the pot. Wasn't long after that I could turn down the heat and put it on "drink mode". I had already put a couple more drinks down by then, don't underestimate my multitasking capabilities. Around 4:00pm, I was looking at recovery centers online and keeping the tabs open on places I thought were interesting when I noticed my drink was just about empty. So, I got up and walked over to the stove, gave a little stir to make sure nothing was sticking, and grabbed the bottle to make another drink. That fifth of 100-proof rum was empty. "Oh shit! I can't believe I drank the bottle. I didn't drink the bottle. I don't remember pouring it empty when preparing my last drink. I'm alone in here though. Did I spill somewhere? There is no mess. I'm all alone in here! It has to be me. Shit!" I downed the rest of what was in my cup, turned the stove off so it wouldn't get ruined, and got my ass to bed. "Maybe I can sleep for a little while and I'll be good when she gets home. She will be so happy I cooked a delicious meal and I have the recovery center tabs still open on my computer. Yeah. She will see those things and she will be okay with knowing I drank this afternoon. Yeah. Shit I let myself down, though."

I woke up to a bright bedroom. I was in it alone, but heard familiar sounds coming from the living room. I couldn't believe I just napped for a couple of hours but it felt like I just closed my eyes for a minute. "I must have napped for only a couple hours. The daylight isn't bright enough to be any other time of day but dusk. I'll slowly get up and scope out the situation in the living room. I bet my wife is relaxing with a bowl of that gumbo!" As I pulled the sheets down to slide out of bed, I noticed I wasn't wearing clothes. I frequently slept naked so it wasn't completely strange to me. I still had a bad feeling, though. The wife must have heard me rustling around because she entered the room at that point. She calmly asked me if I had any memory of the previous evening. I was still trying to figure out what she was talking about. I thought I just took a nap. Well before I got any further clues as to what time or day I was waking up to, she informed me of my Friday night activities. "Oh shit, I slept all night." She said, "Yes you were passed out when I got home yesterday. At least you didn't leave the stove on to burn the apartment complex down. You didn't stay in bed though." My mind started really racing. It was racing in a wet brain sort of state though. She continued, "You got out of bed around 8:30pm and went out on the balcony, naked. You stayed there long enough for someone to see you, grab an apartment manager, and take pictures! You caused the biggest ruckus trying to get back in the apartment and I had to let you inside. I got notice there will be a formal complaint turned in tomorrow and we may only have three days until an eviction. What am I supposed to do with our daughter? Where am I supposed to go?" I was in a shocked and confused state. She was emotional, scared, and so angry. She had every right to feel these things. We hadn't even fully moved in the place and alcohol already caused me to ruin things.

I knew she was justified in every ill feeling towards me. My actions didn't show my thoughts and feelings. I got defensive as I always did after I screwed up. I turned the argument back on her and the way I thought she was frustrating me. I'm talking real problems of the relationship. Most were caused by poor decisions due to drinking, but I refused to acknowledge it when I knew it anyways. I forget who first mentioned the idea, but I distinctly remember her saying, "I think you should leave."

That's all I needed to set me off. "Fuck this! I'm not staying anywhere I'm not wanted!" I put a bag together, kissed my daughter, and I was out the door. I threw my bags in the truck, sat in the driver's seat, turned the key and "oh damn"! I looked down at the ignition interlock and was immediately scared. "Can I even leave? Fuck me! I'm going to have to sit in this thing for hours!" I was yelling in my truck thinking alcohol had to still be in my system. "Fuck it, let's see how long I have to sit and wait on this piece of shit." I blew and passed the breath test. "Well that was uneventful." I told myself while pulling out of my parking spot.

While driving through Houston, I tried to convince myself I was leaving to help my wife and daughter. "If I leave, the apartment manager won't make them leave. I caused a problem, not them. They have to be sympathetic toward a young mother." I wasn't sure what to do but I knew I wanted to disappear for a couple of days.

I found myself pulling up to a hotel on the west side of Houston. I stayed there regularly while working as a drilling trainee a few years ago. I used some hotel points and settled in to a room. I stayed two nights and the entire stay was a blur. It felt like a dream. I went to the store after unloading my truck. I got my soft drinks and a half gallon to hold me over for a while. The hotel had a sports bar in the lobby and a restaurant in the parking lot. I was good on food and now good on my drinks. I didn't leave the hotel until it was time to check out.

I think it was the first night I drunkenly went down the list on a call out website. I must have dialed fifty numbers before someone finally agreed to come meet me. My frustration grew constantly with each denial. I paced the room for what felt like hours before I received a knock on my door. "Oh my God, is this real? Am I really doing this? My wife hates me. My marriage is over. Alcohol is not making me feel any better. Maybe this is a solution." I opened the door and there was a young lady with a smile on her face. It felt so good to have someone look happy to see me. I hadn't put a smile on anyone's face in such a long time. I knew that all of these negative things occurring around me were alcohol induced but I didn't care. I knew her smile and anything we were about to share were all fake. Irrelevant! It was all about me and my feelings. "Come in pretty lady. What's your name?" She gave me a name to call her but I immediately forgot. We made small talk for a while. I'm sure she knew I was drunk and I knew she was full of shit. All that said, I was content being with someone that didn't care. She stayed for a few hours and gave me exactly what I was looking to receive in a temporary euphoria. I walked her out and my night was over, except I lost whatever buzz my bottle gave me earlier that day. "Time for another drink!"

I remember dreams of meeting a woman in the sports bar downstairs one evening. She spent most of the night with me. I honestly don't know if it actually happened. It would have been the second night. I know I went down to the sports bar looking to chat with people and have a good meal. I had drinks for a while down there too. But, I finished off the half gallon of rum I bought the day before and I can't think I realistically picked up a woman at the bar and she came to my room with me. I was in no state of mind to do successfully do that. I just don't know. The dream felt real, but...

Monday morning, I received a phone call from the wife and she told me that we had to be out of the apartment by midnight. I told her I would be there to get our things, but she insisted I take only some of our things I could use at our house. She had things lined up with her cousins. They were helping her move in with her cousin and her kids. She wanted me to stop by there long enough to load a small trailer of items I needed to live and hit the road to Louisiana. I agreed to do as she asked, with one exception. I had to make up excuses because I drank so damn much over the past couple days. I couldn't pass a breath test in my truck to start it. I passed the time at the hotel and ended up leaving that afternoon. I picked up an enclosed rental trailer and went to the apartment. She had her mom packing things up while she was at work and most of the apartment was already boxed when I arrived. It didn't take long for us to load my little trailer. She told me she didn't want me there to help her finish moving. I took a moment with tears in my eyes as I hugged my daughter and got in my truck. I left the apartment complex as her cousins with a large enclosed trailer parked. I was too full of shame to stop and thank them for helping her deal with what I caused. I drove off and headed to Louisiana.

House to Myself

The drive back to Louisiana seemed to drag in the weirdest way. I would lose track of where I was in the drive and I was almost scared of what I would see when I got there. I stopped at my favorite super market and picked up a few groceries since I knew there was nothing in the house. You know I picked up my favorite beverages as well. I had a full day of unpacking a trailer the next day so I could afford to drink for a while that night. Besides, it would help me sleep on the miserable old couch that's in the house.

I arrived to a dark house at night. No lights were on in the place and nothing much moving around. My neighbors were quiet and their subtle porch lights gave a nice glow at the end of the street around my place. After backing up in the driveway, I hopped out and went inside to turn on some lights. I drank a fifth of my favorite rum that night and don't remember much of the details. I just remember sitting under the carport lights, smoking cigarettes and putting my drinks down with country music playing on my phone. I didn't take anything out of the truck or trailer except perishable food and alcohol.

Waking up the next morning wasn't as bad as I anticipated. I probably still had a buzz and I knew I had to work all day. It would wear off slowly so I shouldn't expect a hangover. I couldn't drink because I needed the alcohol out of my system to pass the interlock and return the rented trailer to the local store. So, a sandwich for breakfast with a big sports drink and I was ready to start unpacking. I didn't bother changing clothes or cleaning up.

So, the contents of the trailer weren't very organized. I didn't even know what was in some of the boxes as my wife's mother packed them. I was so uncomfortable and out of my skin while at the apartment with them, I got out as fast as I could. Well, my wife was also telling me she didn't want me there. Anyways, I'll move on. The day of unpacking went well, except I was missing parts and pieces to things. I had my television, but only half of the wall mount. I had my bed, but was missing part of the frame supports. I had a few dishes and mix matched clothes. I had sheets for the bed but no comforter.

I had no money to buy anything I needed because I emptied my account to make sure her and my daughter had money to get by without me around. I knew I had a few hundred dollars before maxing out my credit card.

That had to last me for a week and get me to the heliport so I could go to work.

I got the trailer back where it needed to be returned just in time and made a quick stop for another bottle of alcohol. Things were okay, not good, but okay. I knew I'd have a few drinks while hooking up the cable TV and... Oh wait, I couldn't afford to get it hooked back up so I would just go back to the house and sit there drinking while listening to music on my phone and checking stuff out on social media. I was sure looking forward to that! Okay a little sarcasm, but I had a fresh bottle and no one to give me a hard time about it! The alcoholic in me, my demon on back, convinced me it really was something to be excited about. Imagine that!

The next few days, until the weekend, went the same. I repeated the same activities every day. Drink all night, chill at the house until I could pass the interlock and start my truck, go to the store and get more alcohol. I tried a couple different kinds of whiskey and rum just to liven things up. I even got some beer for in between or day drinking. I barely spoke to my wife. I don't remember any conversations with her over these days.

The only part of the weekend that went well was visiting my parents. I hadn't felt so much love in months.

We prayed. We cried. We had real talks. We laughed. It was a great Sunday visiting them. I left that afternoon to get back to my house and put down a fifth of alcohol because it was my last chance to drink without getting in trouble with work. After such a wonderful day filled with love and prayer, I could only think about going back in seclusion to entertain the very demon that got me in my current state. Wow!

Monday, as usual, was my recovery day. I hung around the house most of the day and called my rig to speak with my relief. He and I had our handover note conversation. I decided to pack up and stay at a hotel near the heliport that night. It was full of benefits. I could watch television, have a good meal, and even have a drink. I figured out that I could drink a pint of whiskey with dinner if I finished it before 7:00 pm and still blow .000 BAC at 5:00 am when I needed to leave in the morning. It was funny though; I got nervous that night and poured out some of the pint just so I wouldn't drink the whole bottle. Dinner was good at the hotel; I went to bed, woke up the next morning and went to work offshore acting like nothing crazy was going on in my life.

I don't remember many details of my hitch offshore this go around. I remember my anxiety being so extreme, it was unreal. Leadership on the rig would ask me to work over or help at night when they were short on management. I felt so empowered. I worked almost 24 hours a day. I couldn't sleep anyways and my job was the only thing I had going good in my life. My bosses were impressed by my work and were giving me more responsibilities. I was also taking everything they would throw my way because I knew the end of the rig contract was getting near. I didn't want to lose my job in a competitive environment. I spoke with my wife daily, but I could feel things changing. We were trying to act somewhat normal when I had the feeling we were already over. Oh yeah, she was planning my daughter's first birthday party while I was offshore. It was going to be at her family's house in Texas and I was going to be there a day before to prepare. This was all going to take place a couple of days after the end of my hitch.

I got back to the house in Louisiana and nothing much changed on my end. I was wanting a better life and to be free of alcohol. I wanted it so bad, but I continued to repeat the same mistakes. Two weeks of working offshore in an alcohol-free environment, easy stuff. Driving home from the heliport without stopping to get a bottle, impossible! I repeated the same routine for a couple of days, talking to my wife in the meantime. We really just talked about the birthday party coming up.

Friday came around and it was time for me to head to Texas. Oh boy! Yes, that's sarcasm. I hated that drive! Traffic always pushed the right buttons. So, what did I do about it? I was cooking a gumbo for the party and had to get good, Cajun ingredients. While I was at the store, I grabbed a bottle of rum. Hey, I was being responsible though. I grabbed a pint so I would only have enough to take the edge off if traffic really got to me. It would fix my mood so I wouldn't be an aggravated asshole when seeing her and her family.

I hit the interstate with my truck loaded up for the day to follow. I had my personal pots and burners in the back, my groceries on the back seat, and my little bottle stashed away. This drive was sort of special in another way as well. I had a stop to make at a shop for truck parts. Remember? I always based my self-esteem on my custom vehicles. It was a quick stop; I grabbed my parts, and was back on the road. Why is this relevant? This selfish pit stop put me driving in the worst afternoon traffic the city had to offer. I quickly went from a decent mood with a little excitement from picking up my stuff, to boiling mad. I started blaming the traffic, my wife, her family, anyone, and anything but myself. The thought never crossed my mind that it wouldn't have gone that way if I would have just had the parts shipped to my house. I wanted to go there and pick them up. I wanted it!

So, I arrived at the house a few minutes after speaking with my wife on the phone. She warned me her dad hadn't gotten back from work yet and I would be waiting a few minutes. She had quite a drive left too. I actually didn't mind being the first one there. It gave me time to sit in my truck and drink that pint to wind down. "I can drink a pint and no one knows I had anything alcoholic to drink." I'd tell myself over and over. I did it so many times before and no one ever said anything. This time was no different. We had a fairly good evening, considering. We visited and the ladies started baking. They decorated cupcakes and other sweets. I don't remember much more of that evening. I think I went to bed early that night. I was an emotional wreck with everything I had done the past months bottled up. I had no one I could talk to, or so I thought.

The next day arrived before I knew it. I was up and unpacking the truck to set up burners and everything else. I had to go to the store for some last-minute groceries and was happy for the opportunity. "I know just where to go!"

There was a decent enough grocery store about fifteen minutes away. I liked this store because it had a liquor store too. So, away I went to get my supplies. It didn't take me long to get everything I needed and I stashed a fifth in my truck for safe keeping. It was a "just in case" kind of thing. I convinced myself I'd need a drink or two while cooking to handle all the people.

Back at the house, I was ready to light the fire. I kept an ice-cold soda at my side throughout the day. I always liked having something to sip on, but it helped chase my occasional swig on this day. I had my gumbo pot on the burner and set up on the back porch. This secluded me a little bit and allowed me direct access to my truck. All I had to do was pass through a gate in the back yard. If anyone asked why I was going to my truck, I'd tell them it was to smoke a cigarette. I didn't want to smoke near the food or the kids. It all made sense to me. I started cooking mid-morning and the party wasn't until about two o'clock that afternoon. It was going to be so good! And, I was happy sitting outside tending to my gumbo while everyone else was in the house visiting and doing their thing.

Guests started arriving shortly after noon. My family even got there early to spend extra time with my daughter. They didn't get to see their grand-daughter much. My gumbo was simmering. I was in a great mood by that time. I drank over half my fifth but I was pacing myself with a swig from the bottle here and there. I had it under control. We had a great party for my girl that afternoon and guests nearly finished off my gumbo. It was a big hit! I didn't associate with most of the guests. I couldn't figure out how to be "fake". I couldn't act like everything was okay. I was dying inside and no one knew it. I snuck away a few more times later that afternoon to drink from my bottle, my evil friend. I had a good day drinking around everyone and I controlled it. They didn't suspect a thing because I didn't get confronted about it. Yup, I did a good job.

We finished off the rest of the gumbo that night while watching football games. I finished off my bottle just before dark. The excuses to go to my truck just kept on coming. After the party, I started cleaning all my supplies and packing to leave the next day. This made it easy for me to make multiple trips to my truck and drink each time. I was at the bottom of the bottle before I knew it. Proud of myself, I relaxed on the couch and watched football with everyone before going to bed with my wife and daughter. I know I didn't get belligerent that day, but I did have enough to drink to fail in remembering the fine details of the day. I have to look at the photo album to help myself remember that day. I don't remember which teams played in that football game that night. I really have something to be proud of, don't I?

I said "Good Bye" to everyone the next day just before lunch and left for Louisiana. You can probably guess what I did next. I stopped at the same usual stores. I drank the same usual drinks. I sat at home watching TV, searching the internet, and keeping myself secluded from the world. There was one difference this go around. I was researching this addiction center that hit heavily on the idea of addiction being a disease and enforcing the need for medication in the journey to recover. I was starting to look at myself as someone with a chronic disease. I was also drinking this whole time and fighting with my wife. The only time I would see my family is when I could drive to Texas.

I reluctantly made reservations at a hotel the following weekend to see my wife and daughter. I drove through a horrible rain storm that Friday afternoon and was emotionally drained by the time I got to my hotel. My "crutch" pint bottle was in my bag so I downed it before I even got out of my truck. I figured my nerves were settled as I checked in and went to my room. I called my wife to let her know I had made it safely and she could come over.

She showed up half an hour later and was alone. She expected to see me drinking and didn't want to put my daughter around me if that were the case. "How dare she do this bullshit?" It pissed me off so badly. I was going through so much to see them and she didn't even want to see me! I spent so much time and money driving back and forth. I was spending so much on hotels. I was giving her money on top of all my expenses. I just wanted to feel loved and spend time with my daughter. She couldn't tell I drank when I got there. No one ever accused me of drinking when I "only drank a pint". She accused me of drinking, of course. She told me she was leaving and wasn't coming back with my daughter because she could tell I drank. I accused her of showing up with that mindset and falsely accusing me of drinking. She left and I went down to the sports bar to drink my night away. My weekend was ruined "because she had it in her mind I would be drinking before she showed up" and I won't stand for that shit.

My wife and daughter showed up the next morning to visit. She wanted to spend the day with me. "Why the fuck would I want to do something like that? You didn't want to spend time together last night. You showed up without my daughter, knowing I wanted to see her more than you!" I felt like I had to say something like that to hurt her. She needed to feel bad for showing up under the assumption I had been drinking. It didn't matter if she was right, I couldn't let her know she was right. We hung out until it was checkout time and then I left for Louisiana. She was given that time only because I knew I had to stay put that long for last night's alcohol to leave my system. I was still operating under the "I don't want to be around anyone that doesn't want to be around me" mindset that started when I left the apartment.

I made it home and resumed drinking. I had movies to watch, bottles to drink, and food in the fridge. I even made some calls through a local website and found someone to come over to the house and "hang out". I really got a woman to come spend a few hours with me in a house with a torn up, run down couch, a TV on the floor, and a mattress on the floor of the bedroom with only a sheet on it. This is literally all I had and I bullshitted my way through the night talking gibberish of how I just started moving in that day. I explained that I just moved there from Texas and starting a new life and all this other crap I can't remember. She either ate it up or put on a damn good act for her money. She made me feel just like I wanted to feel. She complimented me and pointed out all of the positive points of my house. She made small talk in between everything else. She temporarily filled my void and then she left. So I had a few more drinks while remembering how good she made me feel about myself.

I woke up the Sunday morning feeling decent from the night before. I didn't have any remorse for what I had done. I felt like I was fending for myself when no one else would. With Sunday being my last chance to drink, I decided to set my floor mounted TV to the football games and get some food to cook. I'd spend the day doing my favorite things that didn't cost much money.

I was back in business after a quick drive to the grocery store. I got some chicken and sausage to make a small gumbo and some stovetop rice since I hadn't found my rice cooker. I knew she kept it on purpose, but whatever. I also made sure to get myself a bottle of my favorite rum. I stood in the alcohol section of the store, staring at the bottles for what seemed to be and hour. I wanted the half gallon so bad! But I knew two days would be needed to clean my system and I didn't have that much time before I had to go to work. I reluctantly decided on the fifth of 100-proof rum. It would give me more than a regular fifth, but less than a half-gallon of the standard 70 proof rum I drank every day. I was happy with my compromise and headed back home. Oh, it helped that I still had beer in the refrigerator at home. Ya know? Just in case I needed a little more.

I started cooking and watching football. And drinking... I did more drinking than anything else. I let the amount of drink in my cup decide whether I was in the kitchen to stir the pot or in the living room watching the game. I was doing what I wanted and for the moments spent alone in the house that afternoon, I was happy. I was happy for what I remember of that afternoon. I passed out shortly after turning off the stove. I don't remember watching any of the three o'clock games.

The next day was full of cleaning my mess and sobering up so I could leave for work. I repeated the cycle over again. I cleaned the house through and through. The whole pot of food I cooked the day before was still sitting on the stove. I got to throw that out in the trash. "I waste so much money on food." I thought to myself while throwing it away. "I need to stop cooking so much while I'm drinking." Everything was done mid-afternoon and I was ready to head to the hotel for crew change the next day.

I took the opportunity to work offshore an extra week. I was trying to spend as much time offshore because I knew it would keep me sober and would also make me some extra money to try and keep up with all the bills my wife and I were stacking up. It was a win-win situation. I knew that I needed to stay offshore as much as possible for the rest of the year. I had to get by because I couldn't start my treatment until my appointment after the first of the year. Remember that save all place I mentioned? I was infatuated with the place. I was on the website every day while offshore. I started going through a workbook I got from their website. I read all about their treatment and how they were going to heal me. I was so excited! I was also continuing to excel at work. The rig needed more than ever. The contractor's management came out to the rig and told all their workers that they would be let go, laid off at the end of contract. That was about a 60-day notice to their employees. It was also right in the middle of a very important project for their client. I finished my hitch concentrating on everything going on and barely talking to my wife. I told her that she would have to come to see me on my next days off if she cared and wanted to spend time together. She agreed and we made plans for my birthday because it was during my next time at the house. I was excited, but somewhat on edge as to whether or not it would happen. I had a feeling she would find a reason not to make the drive to see me.

I made it home to our place in Louisiana filled with anxiety about the upcoming week. Would I see my family? Did I matter enough for my wife to go through the trouble of driving to me? She had already warned me she didn't want to go back to our house so I talked to my family about spending the weekend with them. They always loved to have us over so they could play with their only granddaughter. They loved seeing my wife and I, but my little girl stole the show. We didn't get that far, so I'll get on with my story. I don't remember speaking with my wife the first day off the rig. That doesn't mean we didn't speak, I had my usual to drink that afternoon and evening. We spoke the next day and she warned me she wasn't coming. Her grandmother was sick and she was going to spend a few days with her. It proved to be her last days. Did I care? NO! All I cared about was the fact my wife wouldn't go out of her way to see me. I concentrated on the fact that she wouldn't come to see me. I wasn't enough for her. I wasn't her family. Her family was in Texas. I kept rolling these things over and over in my mind while finding the bottom of glass bottles. A few days of this and she told me her grandmother died. She gave me the information for the funeral services and asked me to be there. She still wanted me there after all the grief I had been giving her through these events. My drinking continued to get away from me and I drank nearly a half-gallon of whiskey the night before her grandmother's funeral. I woke up the next morning early enough to leave and make the funeral service, but sober enough to know I was still too drunk to get out of the house. How did I handle the situation? I talked down to her on the phone and made it out to be her fault. I acted as I was hurt and too emotional to attend anything. I think I even accused her of faking everything as if she made up the story of a family member dying so she didn't have to see me.

I didn't see my family at all while home this stretch. I was sticking to what I said about not driving to Texas. We all paid for it too. My daughter didn't see her father. My wife didn't see her husband. I stayed home drinking for almost two weeks straight. I started drinking so much at one point, I didn't ever sober up to start my truck and drive to the store. I convinced myself I was exercising and walked to a corner store for alcohol each day. My truck went almost a week without being started. Equipped with sports shorts, light tee shirt, running shoes, I looked the part of any local in the neighborhood concerned about their health. The difference was my agenda. The first day I walked to the store, I started down my street and timed myself. It was at least a mile for the round trip and took me over forty five minutes. The second day, well the second day was interesting. I figured out I could get the walk done in less than thirty minutes by jumping the fence in my back yard. I could climb it leaving my house, but there was nothing to help me climb it coming back. Regardless, I was happy with the short cut. My shopping bag usually contained a big beer for the walk back, one or two fifths of hard liquor, and either a pint of something else or a box of beer. I'd smile and wave at people in the neighborhood on my way back home figuring no one knew any better because of my attire. Forget that I had a tall beer in my hand and a bag full of alcohol! These walks usually took place between ten and eleven o'clock in the morning. The afternoons and evenings were comprised of enjoying my consumables, chasing the bottom of one bottle after another. Once Monday came around, I turned it off and went back to work.

At this point, Christmas wasn't far away. I was spending Christmas offshore again, five or six years in a row now. My marriage was another story. I couldn't figure out which way it was going, but I knew things didn't feel right. My wife agreed to make the drive over and visit with me since she was spending all the holidays with her family and I would be closing out the year by spending all the holidays at work. I wasn't sure of any other motives she may have had for coming visit and I didn't care. I was getting Christmas for New Years and I was happy.

We had a good visit for the five or so days my wife came to see me. I tried my best to leave alcohol alone. It felt like a win for me by only getting inebriated two days while she was in town. Well, it felt that way to me. No one else around me saw it that way. I out did myself the day before she drove in to see me to hopefully take the edge off. I managed most of the time by drinking a half pint to a pint each day. No one would ever accuse me of drinking while I stuck to that amount. BUT...... I went to get breakfast for everyone one morning in town and stopped by the store to pick up some vodka. I bought some juice to mix with it and ended up saving the juice for my egg sandwich. The warm glass of the pint bottle pressed to my lips offered no consolation as I swallowed its contents in seconds. My family ate a good breakfast as I slept most the day. After waking up, I isolated myself until the next morning so I wouldn't have to deal with the uncomfortable conversations.

I mention isolation, but that was only from my parents. My wife and I spoke. I mean, we were sleeping in the same bed. She used the usual tone of voice she had been using when we talked things over. I could never quite decide if it was disappointment or anger. She was slipping away from me though. She had enough and I could tell, so I mentioned my plans of meeting with a counselor at their first availability after New Year's Day. I had to say something to get her attention and it worked. She needed to see I was doing something more than talking about getting help. My actions showed very different things from my intentions. I was that guy talking a good game and saying all the right things while repeating the same mistakes over and over again. The things I was doing remained unseen as I was separated from my family and isolated in a house a state away. She agreed to stay through the day I had my appointment and I was so excited. Her knowing I had made the plans gave relief and I was on an emotional high knowing I meant enough for her to make the appointment with me.

We made that appointment as expected and it seemed to go well. I even started outpatient counseling that night. I didn't expect for things to happen that quick. I thought I'd have a couple more days to drink and say my farewell to the demon. That's not what these counselors had in mind. They put me on the spot and pressured me to stay at their place to attend my first session of counseling. They also started the drug and alcohol screening process with me. They explained how it all worked through urinalysis. I agreed to start testing and told them I drank a day or two before sitting in front of them. They said it didn't matter and first tests were expected to fail. They explained that they needed to see the levels of alcohol in my system to correctly prescribe the medication I needed. That's right, they also explained how I would need to be on long term medication to stabilize my brain and live a healthy life. My wife and I ate all the bullshit they fed us and I was on cloud nine. I'm going to get healed at this place!

Healing Process

My wife left the place and I remained over there for my first session. The place intrigued me. Something gave me a weird vibe about this particular treatment center, though. Was it a legitimate feeling or was it my alcoholic mind telling me to haul ass out of there? I was unsure and stuck it out. I did so well, I deserved a drink before bed! Right? Well I convinced myself the alcohol screenings wouldn't clear up before I went back to work anyways. I stopped by one of my favorite corner stores and got a bottle. It was a quick supper and then I was set for drinking on the couch while watching movies. I don't remember what was playing when I passed out, but woke up that next morning with a little bit of rum left in the bottle next to the couch. I rolled over and turned the television back on to the morning news. Something about that bottle next to the couch was distracting me. It didn't take five minutes for me to grab the bottle and drink the rest of the rum. Thirty or so minutes after that, I found myself grabbing a beer from the refrigerator. Well, what now? I convinced myself that it didn't matter if I failed all the tests this week. I decided to keep drinking and attend the remaining two sessions of the week. I knew I'd fail the tests but that wouldn't matter. It would be a fresh start when I got back from offshore. I'd be free from alcohol and it would be easy to get on track!

Okay so back to what I was actually doing that Tuesday morning. I had a cold beer open and sitting on the counter next to me as I brushed my teeth. I had a couple more while getting dressed. Then I headed out of the house for my morning walk. You remember my morning exercise routine? Yeah, I jumped the fence in my back yard and hiked to the corner store. I got myself a big beer for the walk home and a fifth of vodka for the house. I didn't get any more because I knew I wouldn't have been able to sober up before my counseling session Wednesday night. That was going to be an important night for me, because my wife and daughter would be driving in to attend. Wednesdays were family nights and she agreed, with the support of her boss, to attend every Wednesday. I searched for the bottom of that vodka bottle all day and most of the night, only to wake up Wednesday and wait for my wife while sobering up.

She made it that evening and we had a decent session. They discussed the anatomy of the brain and chemical processes involved with drug use. It was an informative session, but I didn't feel like we got much out of it. There was something missing. We were looking for more of a counseling session than "How Stuff Works" lecture. Still, I was happy my wife showed enough love for me to drive and attend.

The next morning was included breakfast at home while she did a little work and I played with my daughter. I didn't drink after the session and I stuck with my family. We enjoyed each other's company for a while and I left my family's house when she left for Texas. I stopped to get some groceries and something to cook myself that night before arriving to my house. I walked back and forth, looking at the liquor section from a safe distance. I almost made it to check out when I noticed a beautiful display for some special reserve whiskey. I had to try it! Well, I had already convinced myself the urinalyses given to me that week would be dirty. Now, I was going to spend the next four days alone at home so there was no good reason for me to stay sober. My song of drinking and self-destruction was stuck on repeat until I left for work offshore the following Monday afternoon.

I made it to the rig and started my hitch with an uneasy feeling. We started taking things down as the contract was in its final days. I helped pack all of my client's belongings to send off to another rig that was still working. I wasn't told anything about my future working with the company. They gave me excellent reviews, but low market prices were shutting down drilling projects across the world. My wife and I tried to talk through our personal issues while I dealt with the anxiety of losing my job on my own. Don't get me wrong, I mentioned it to her. I didn't emphasize anything too much though. She shouldn't be worrying about that when she had so much other stuff on her mind. The hitch went by quickly as we stayed busy handling operations while still rigging down. The air was heavy. Emotions were all over the place. Some crew members had already received new assignments. Others were waiting on word from upper management. I was one of the others. I finished my hitch with a smile on my face and kept a positive attitude. My emotions were stable and I was strong, until I got to my vehicle and drove away from the heliport. I was finally alone and wouldn't be bothered. An overwhelming feeling came across me as thoughts about my career and marriage both ending soon flooded my mind. I broke down emotionally and cried much of the way home that day.

The house was cold with such an empty feeling when I arrived. I walked through the place as I would usually do before settling down. I was always worried that someone may be in the home or something. I'd get back to a home that was supposed to be empty for at least two weeks. Better be safe than sorry.

So, the last thing I checked in the house was the refrigerator. I made a quick list of groceries I would need, then I looked in the drinks tray and counted the beer I had left. I stared at those cans of cold, crisp beer as my mouth watered. But I wouldn't drink in this moment. "No! I have to go to the store first." I remember saying that aloud as I laughed and proceeded out the door. There was no counseling session that night and I needed to escape from my anxiety. It didn't take much to talk myself into buying a bottle that day. It was the last day I would ever set foot on the rig I worked for over three years. My wife and I spoke briefly that afternoon after I got back from the store. I don't remember what was talked about, but the conversation was short and sweet. Well the sweet part may not be accurate. Our conversations would always leave me feeling more confused and on edge.

The next day was slow passing as I waited for the evening time so I could see my wife and daughter. It was another family night and they were coming to town. I wanted a drink so bad, but I knew I couldn't drink while they were around. We got to the session that night and it was a repeat of the previous week. I was happy to be in the presence of my wife and simultaneously felt horrible because we weren't getting quality family counselling. It is worth mentioning that I was prescribed multiple medications from this place. I was consuming thirteen pills a day. I was willing to do anything to get better and my high hopes for this place allowed them to easily convince me the medication was necessary. I don't even know how exactly the medication affected me at that time. Maybe it had something to do with all of my emotions. Anyways, we enjoyed each other's company that night and I had a good time with my daughter. We spent our morning together the next day before they left for Texas.

I arrived back home to my place that afternoon and was still struggling with staying away from alcohol. I picked up a pint of rum so I could have a couple drinks, but wouldn't get drunk. I stuck to it and went to bed that evening feeling like I achieved something. I held myself to the amount I planned to drink. It didn't matter how I accomplished the goal, it was done according to plan. The next few days were quiet at home, except for my session Friday. I went to the morning group so my Friday evening would be open. I was considering a drive to Texas to see my family, but that fell through. So, the weekend was once again spent alone in an empty house. I know, it's the perfect environment for someone trying to overcome addiction. I drank some that weekend, but I didn't get drunk each day. I kept buying small bottles. That was the only thing controlling the amount I'd drink. It could be a half pint or a half gallon; I was going to find the bottom of the bottle. Things were progressively getting more dangerous for me as the days passed. I was alone drinking while taking all the medication that was prescribed. I stayed out of trouble as long as the bottles stayed small.

EtG Urine Test

EtG Urine Alcohol Test checks for Ethyl Glucuronide, which is present in the body for three days after drinking alcohol. This test is often ordered in child custody cases, or whenever a person is required to be completely abstinent.

When someone consumes alcohol (ethanol), the body metabolizes it at the rate of approximately one drink per 90 minutes. However, once the alcohol is gone, a side product of the body's metabolization, known as ethyl glucorinide, remains. This metabolite stays in the urine for about 3 days after the consumption of alcohol.

All was lost after the weekend. I was confronted by a counselor on Monday morning when I showed up for a session. We spoke for a while and he let me know that my tests were still showing levels of ethyl glucuronide in my urine. That confrontation was not received well. I sat through my session and instead of taking it as a "wake up call" to stop drinking, I got a bottle of 100 proof on the way home. I was drinking for lunch! That bottle was enough alcohol to send me over the edge, too. I hadn't drunk that much since prescribed the medication. I took the medicine exactly as prescribed, even on this day. And, the next thing I remember was fighting with my wife on the phone the Wednesday afternoon. See, she knew I had been drinking and called me out on it. She also decided not to come over to attend a session together, due to my drinking. We had talked the Monday and Tuesday multiple times and it wasn't good. I only know that because she told me about it later. I was drunk and a selfish asshole.

It could go without saying, but I'll talk about it anyways. There was no session for me that Wednesday night. I stayed home drinking the rest of my alcohol and ate leftovers. I ignored all calls and text messages, except the occasional text from the wife that would set me off. Any reply I'd send was gibberish. It's a wonder why she would even attempt to get in touch with me.

The next day involved a trip to the store to stock up. My mind was flooded with so many thoughts. I didn't care anymore. I bought a fifth of whiskey, half gallon of my favorite rum, couple bottles of wine, and a case of beer. Then, I went to the side of the store with food and bought everything I needed to cook a gumbo. I figured I could cook a pot and eat from it for a few days. I was ready for the weekend. Ha, yeah.

I got home and didn't finish unloading the truck before making a drink. My mind was set. I screwed up already so I'd see how far I could go. I remember drinking beer and some of the half gallon while cooking my gumbo. Next, I woke up Friday morning with the stove top still on low. The full pot of gumbo was still sitting on top and I was reaching for the rum. I put the half gallon to my lips and flipped the bottle upside down. With a few ounces swallowed, I cracked open a cold beer and drank it too. "Now I'm ready to get my day started! Let's see what this gumbo tastes like." Yeah, I had gumbo for breakfast with rum and coke on the side. Needless to say, I wasn't going anywhere or getting anything done that day. I drank that morning until I passed out. After getting a couple hours of sleep, I woke up to resume drinking. That process was repeated over and over again. I'd wake up in the middle of the night and drink until I fell back asleep. By Saturday morning, I drank a fifth of whiskey, half gallon of rum, and most of the beer. "Off to the store! I have to stock back up."

This trip involved deli sandwiches and other easy meals. I didn't have much interest in eating. "Let's grab a case of beer and a half gallon of rum. Uh, I'll get some vodka too." I even got a bag of ice so I didn't have to worry about my ice maker keeping up.

I got back to the house to see nothing changed. I forgot to lock the door though. So in my state of light paranoia, I gave the house a good walk through and checked every space to make sure no one was there. Yea, I didn't mention paranoia before. I'd regularly check windows, door locks, empty rooms of the house, and the yard. I got up in the middle of the night once with a flood light on so I went outside with a kitchen knife thinking someone had to be back there. Ha, nothing. I'd stare down my street through the mini blinds on the living room windows. It's like I had a constant feeling someone or something was coming to get me. I didn't want to be taken by surprise. Oh, insanity.

So my walk through was done and I was enjoying my first drink. Some groceries were put up in the kitchen, others sat on the counter. It didn't matter, I was content. I decided to order a movie on pay per view. I scrolled through the list and decided to watch a movie. "Cool, let's buy it. Wait, why isn't it giving me the purchase option? What the hell?!?! Oh! I bought this movie yesterday. I bought this movie yesterday?" Sure did. I wasn't even mad though. I didn't remember anything about the movie, not even buying it. I looked at it like I was getting a free movie. The rest of my Saturday was spent between the couch and the kitchen. I was either drinking or making another one.

Sunday was another day to see just how much I could drink. It was the end of playoffs and I was going to watch the games. Something came over me where I got the desire to drink a specific alcohol this day. I still had rum, whiskey, and beer left but something was calling me. Oh yeah, I drank all the vodka and wanted more to mix with juice. "Let's get to the store!"

I went to the closest store, forgetting it was Sunday morning. They wouldn't sell me anything because that parish had a law against selling alcohol before noon on Sundays. No problem, I lived close to the parish line and knew where to go. There was a store located a few miles away and they had a good selection of liquor. I could taste the first drink while cruising down the narrow, two lane back road which lead me to the store. If I didn't already have any signs telling me it was a bad idea, I got a good one half way down the road. I was crossing a small bridge when a truck pulled on the road from my left. It crossed in my lane as it was attempting to straighten up and I panicked. I swerved to the right and the rear passenger side of my truck hit the cement wall of the bridge. It wasn't a violent event and I didn't notice anything different about the way my truck drove. "Oh well, let's get to that store so I can get home." I wasn't worried one bit. I got my drink and got my ass back home. Never went out of my way to look at the damage. That could wait.

Back at home, I was pre-gaming and enjoying my drink. I wasn't talking to my wife so my phone was quiet. It was just me and my old demon. Repeating some of the same routines, I drank till passing out and woke up to continue drinking. I couldn't get enough alcohol in my body.

At some point that afternoon, in my broken state, I called my parents and begged them for help. Phone in hand, dial tone and ringing, I still had the half gallon turned bottom side up. I drank while I spoke to my mom asking for help. I barely remember the conversation, but it stuck with me when my mom said that my dad would be at my house around eight o'clock the next morning. I was crying out of control when we spoke. I cried for a while after we hung up. I was desperate for a change.

All that said, I continued to drink all evening and through the night. I'd stand over the sink and turn the bottle over like I was going to pour out the contents. Yeah, right. I'd bend over to put my mouth to the opening of that cursed bottle. I hated it, but I couldn't part with it.

I somehow woke up at six thirty Monday morning. The half-gallon was sitting next to the couch, within my reach. It had about an inch or more of rum still in it. I didn't lift my head from the pillow before grabbing the bottle and finishing the contents. I drank that rest of that bottle like I needed it to live! The television was turned on next and I walked in the kitchen. I had a small mess with some dishes to clean. A cold beer went well with the chores and I moved on to a shower. I was dressed and had a bag ready before my dad showed up. All of my empty bottles were in the trash for pick up and I was good to go. As I was waiting, pacing back and forth through the house with a beer in my hand, my dad pulled in the driveway. It was a knee jerk reaction to quickly finish the beer and throw it in the trash. I grabbed a soft drink and greeted him at the back door.

Legal Treatment

I opened that door to look into the eyes of a concerned father. My dad always tried to be a stern father. On this day, his eyes were filled with worry. He hugged me and stepped inside my house. I went to grab some of my things I needed and he looked around the place. I knew he was just trying to get an idea of how I was living. The house showed I obviously wasn't living well, but at least I had already thrown out the empty bottles with other trash. I felt like it wasn't so bad with that stuff gone already.

We walked out as I double checked the doors and my truck. I didn't want the truck with me for the next few days. I wanted him to take me away and I knew that I needed to be somewhat captive. I would have bought alcohol the next time I had an opportunity. I knew that to be true. I knew it and I was still buzzing from the alcohol I drank that morning.

We hit the road and went to the same treatment center I had been going to the past few weeks. I wanted to tell them everything and get on the right path. As they listened, I didn't feel any sincerity in their words. My dad even found their suggestions to be bullshit. They pushed more medication and a full thirty plus day inpatient treatment program. I was still willing to go through the inpatient treatment. I was that desperate. The inpatient center was across town from the outpatient office where we were located. So we left and were driving towards the address a counselor gave me when I received a call. "Sir, you are on your way to our facility for inpatient treatment?" I confirmed the gentleman's statement and let him know I was looking forward to getting there. "Sir, you do realize there will be an up-front charge of over two thousand dollars? It will be due on your arrival." I was floored. I wrote down the charges he spoke about and told him I'd call back. My dad pulled over in a parking lot and I got emotional with him. I broke down crying. The morning drinks exaggerated my emotions. I was overwhelmed, none the less. We talked things over for a while and he helped me collect myself. I talked through several different scenarios and he agreed they (my parents) would help me through my recovery. He saw the desperation in my eyes.

I called the treatment center back and told them I wouldn't be doing business with them anymore. I explained my disappointment in their establishment and my reasons for leaving. When I hung up the phone, my dad asked if there was anything else I needed before continuing to their house. "Well, I managed to lose all of my contacts while on my five-day binge drinking excursion. Do you have time to drive me to get my eyes checked? They will update my new prescription and fix me up with some glasses too." My dad agreed. He let me know that he cleared his morning to help me out. I sincerely thanked him and we proceeded to get me checked out. I remember hitting on the optometry technicians while they were working on me. I wasn't vulgar or rude, but I definitely wasn't myself. I'm even surprised I got a good prescription, knowing I wasn't sober. It all worked out somehow and we proceeded to go home. I was looking forward to it, although I knew I had a rough few days ahead. I drank enough alcohol over the past several days to put myself in a grave. Somehow, I made it through a five-day period of drinking several gallons of rum, several fifths of vodka and whiskey, and multiple cases of beer. I knew there was not going to be a hangover. I was about to go through hell with withdrawals. I knew this because I did it to myself many times when sobering up to go to work offshore. What I didn't know was that it was going to be the worst experience of my life. I never drank such an extreme amount in such a short period of time.

We got to the house and I quickly brought my things to the bedroom where I would be sleeping. I crashed on the couch after that and my dad didn't really mess with me.

He knew I wasn't physically well. I put the television on low and acted as if I was going to watch it. My mind was melted. I don't know how else to describe it. Thoughts were racing, yet they were mixed and didn't make sense. Everything was skewed. It wasn't withdrawals yet. It was slightly sobering up. See I had been through the process so many times that I might not have been able to comprehend thoughts of the world around me, but I sure knew where I was in the process by the way my body was functioning. Malfunctioning is probably a better word.

I was tired and weak while my mind was racing. I would get hungry and thirsty, but couldn't tolerate eating or drinking. These symptoms would stick for about twenty-four hours. I got a terrible case of the shakes later that evening. There was no chance of eating dinner with utensils. That was a good sign though. Going through the process, I'd only get the shakes once I was done metabolizing all the alcohol in my system. I was sober for the first time since I got back from work. Trying to sleep was another story. The next several nights would most likely be a series of tossing and turning with little to no actual sleep. I knew this before going to bed that first night, so I told my dad to keep an eye on me. I asked him to check on me from time to time and explained I would leave the bedroom door open with a night light. In efforts to prevent from alarming him, I didn't mention my real concerns. I did my share of research through the years and I showed every sign and symptom of alcohol withdrawals through my adult life. I experienced all of them except seizures. He didn't know how extreme my condition was and I should have been detoxing in a medical facility. That's the truth, but I wasn't paying thousands of dollars out of pocket. I tried to pray while beginning my detox journey at home. I couldn't get further than the opening line of a prayer.

That night wasn't so bad. I could tell my body wasn't regulating temperature quite like it should, but I was managing. I wouldn't shake if I lay still in bed, so I watched a lot of late night television and slept in short naps. The next morning came before I was ready, but no one would come to disturb me in such a fragile state. I continued the cycle through the day.

I still couldn't eat much that day, but water was soothing. Daytime television kept me company while I sat dormant in a recliner. Things started to get interesting that evening. My mom got home and we talked about my options. Something had to happen. I needed help. She talked to me with an open mind and suggested another treatment center. I think she exaggerated some points about the place, but she knew what I needed to hear to get me there. I was so beat down and disappointed by the past treatment center! So what did she tell me? What was so important to me about my service provider? I wanted a counselor that was a recovered addict. I needed someone who understood what I was talking about, not a person who read about it in a text book. I wanted to get with someone who had been beat down, lost everything, and came back stronger than ever. I needed someone to look up to as a mentor and role model. Looking back, I should have dove head first in to Alcoholics Anonymous. Plenty of people fitting that exact description would have helped me for free!

Plans were set for me to set up an appointment the next day. I was still suffering terribly though. And I was beat down so bad from the last experience. There was no excitement or high hopes for this round. I was simply open to try it out.

That night, there was no anxiety about what was to come. I travelled in to the phase of withdrawals (or detox) involving hallucinations and nightmares. My body was starting to allow itself to shut down and sleep. My mind had other plans. While my body cycled between cold sweats and feverish tendencies, my mind was providing vivid dreams. These dreams were twisted views of real situations. The most terrifying episode my mind played came in to tune around three o'clock in the morning. I dozed off while under the covers. The television was on with the volume muted. I mention the covers because I cycled from covers and no covers.

Anyways, I didn't even realize I was sleeping. I suddenly found myself lying on the couch in my old house. The scene was set to be early in the morning, just after sunrise. I sat up on the couch while attempting to turn up the volume on the television. I was looking over to that flat screen sitting on the floor. The news was on. I couldn't hear the news anchors, but somehow knew they were speaking to me. "Shit, I need a drink. Where's my bottle?" I stood up from the couch and went to the kitchen in search for my rum. I didn't see my rum, but I did see a toddler standing in front of the kitchen sink. He was somewhat pale skinned with dark brown hair. An immediate sense of evil came over me. There was something wrong with this child! I turned to go in the pantry, still looking for a bottle. There was a little girl in there when I walked through the door way. She wasn't quite like the boy though. Her limbs were crooked as though her joints weren't properly aligned. I retreated to my couch. As I sat down, a chill came over me and I turned to my left. Another boy! He seemed to be three or four years old and looked normal enough. His brown hair was in a cute, childish bowl haircut. He wore jean shorts with dark suspenders over a white tee shirt. He wouldn't speak as he just stared at me. I was frightened, but could he tell? I grabbed my phone to call for help. The display lit up as I pushed the button and I felt hopeful. I pressed the icons on the screen navigating me to the phone number screen. It went blank. It went blank! "Exit out. I'll exit out and go back in. It's just a glitch." I looked up and the boy had stepped a little closer. "Fuck this!" I told myself while fighting with my phone. "Okay. Phone, key pad, shit its blank again. I know! I'll just go to my address book and dial from there." I went that route and all of my contacts were visible. "Yes! It works! I got it now." I looked up before pressing on my dad's name. The boy was sitting on the couch, next to me. "It's cool. Be calm. He's just a boy." I slowly pressed down on the screen to call out and nothing happened. It was frozen. I slowly looked up and the other two had moved to the doorways. They blocked the open doors, effectively trapping me in the room. I slowly looked left to see the boy on the couch. He never changed his facial expression, but I felt as though he was now smiling. I couldn't take my eyes off of him and I couldn't move. He reached out, pinched my arm, and I woke up. I woke up rubbing my left arm as it hurt. I really felt a pinch and my arm was in pain.

Convincing myself the pinch was due to breaking out in cold sweats under the sheets, I threw the covers off me. I turned to the television and found sit-com reruns to watch. Struggling to stay awake and scared to fall back asleep, I passed out again. I was right back in the old house. There were two more kids in there with me this time. They blocked all exits and I couldn't get my phone to work. I sat and cried on that old couch for what felt like an eternity. Meanwhile, that same little boy came back and sat next to me again. I gave him a quick look and then put my head down. I didn't care anymore. It didn't feel like a dream, but I didn't care anymore! I give up! I felt a light pressure on my left shoulder and center of my back. It tingled as chills ran down my spine. I looked again to see he put his arm on me and was rubbing my shoulder and back. He was consoling me, trying to make me feel better. I was confused as I looked around at the others. They were all standing still, though appeared to have a gentle sway to their stance. As soon as I began feeling an eerie calm in the atmosphere, the boy reached with his left arm and pinched me once again. I woke up panting with an aching left arm once again. No covers were on me this time and I couldn't justify my discomfort. There was no more sleep in my near future.

I stared at the television for hours. It was a quiet house and I had the volume almost muted. The air was heavy and I continued to cycle between cold sweats and heat waves. Eventually, I heard my mom's alarm clock. It sounded for a few seconds and then I heard her shuffling around. I would quickly learn her routine. Noises around the house moved from her bedroom, through the living room, and on to the kitchen. I could hear the coffee maker brewing a moment later. Her trail of sounds followed back to her room and I could hear conversation between my parents shortly after. My dad usually woke up to keep her company as she dressed, but he didn't really get up. Shuffling continued and I heard them say goodbyes for the morning. The house went quiet once the alarm announced an open door. I'd lay there for a couple more hours, watching the fan slowly turn.

I ran into my dad while scuffling to the kitchen. He asked how I was feeling and reminded me to call the treatment center. It was now mid-morning and memories of my childhood were haunting me, preventing me from staying in bed any longer. "Time to get up and get our day started!" "You can't sleep all day!" "Time to be productive!" Statements from my dad during high school summers and college replayed in my mind. But why was my mind resorting back to my juvenile times?

I made "the call" while trying to drink a cup of coffee. My shakes were residing so it was getting easier to complete the simple tasks we all take for granted. I was entering the final stage of my detox. This stage involved excessive mucous production in the back of my throat and sinuses. I coughed precariously during the conversation, but the lady on the other end of the line was undeterred. We set an appointment for the next day and that was it. I had plans and was set to spend the rest of my day coughing and blowing my nose while watching reruns of my favorite sit-coms.

Moving on to that night, I was dealing with chills more than the hot and cold cycles. I was getting to the end of my personal hell. My demon wasn't going quietly, though. Closing my eyes and slipping into the subconscious meant returning to my house. It was just the way I left it, except no demon children were occupying the space this time. People were touring the exterior of the home. A construction crew was working in the front yard. I would move from window to window, looking through the blinds. All the activity was disturbing as I wanted to be left alone. I was hiding inside the house at first, and then something startled me. A group of people were making their way to the back yard. I couldn't deal with that, so I went to the back door to confront them. As I opened the door, I felt a gentle breeze. I exited and walked towards the group. Something gave me a sense of déjà vu. They didn't acknowledge me when I stood in front of them. "Hello! I don't appreciate you on my property." They were involved in a conversation within themselves. I was invisible! I was frantic and went back in the house. The crew in the front yard now had a large excavation hole dug out. "What are they doing?" I tried to figure things out but nothing made sense. I attempted to walk back outside to confront the construction crew. As I crossed the threshold of the back door, a dark figure hit me. I was swept off my feet and woke up when I hit the ground. Everything felt so real, too real. I was lying on my back, just as I should have been lying by the way I was hit. I was in bed, though. I was lying in bed, in the safety of my parent's home. No more sleep for me tonight.

My dad and I headed to the treatment center for my orientation. I was emotionally numb going in to this. We arrived and there was a very short wait before a pleasant lady invited us into her office. We began talking a little and once my dad stopped his small talk, we could get down to business. She asked about my recent history and I gave her details about my previous treatment, as well as my detox over the past few days. She explained how fortunate I was to make it through that experience unsupervised. It wasn't anything new to me. She asked about my treatment and medication. Upon hearing everything I was prescribed, she explained how it caused the extreme relapse. She also explained how the medication should have been a "red flag". I understood what she was telling me as she explained there would be no medication and no treatment by a resident physician. This was interesting. It was the first place I heard of that didn't have a physician or psychologist itching to examine me and give me medication. She and I both agreed the Intensive Outpatient Program would fit me best. I had some paperwork to sign and we were ready to go. My health insurance was going to cover the complete cost of treatment so I had no reason to turn them down. "Let's give this a shot!"

My dad and I left so I could get my truck from my house. I was a few days sober and needed my transportation now that I was going to counseling. I was starting that night!

I thanked him as I exited his truck. He sat still in my driveway as I approached mine. I started it and rolled down the windows to let in some fresh air. I waved goodbye to him and drove away. While backing out of my driveway, I couldn't take it anymore. I had to look at the damage. I stopped at my mailbox so it appeared as though I was checking my mail. I actually went through the motions of going through my mail box. I don't know why I did those things. What was I afraid of? It didn't matter if anyone saw me check out my truck in my driveway, but I still felt as though I needed to hide what I was doing. Anyways, I walked around and found considerable damage to the passenger rear fender, wheel, bumper, and light. I could see all the damage from a few feet away, but it wasn't obvious from a distance. I was relieved to see the tail light still worked too. "Oh well, nothing I can do but try to get it fixed and prevent it from happening again. Let's get to my counselor's office!"

I drove straight back to the treatment center and started reading my treatment guideline. They also gave me a legal disclaimer to read over and get back to them the following week. I did it all. I even signed the papers so they could be returned while walking in to my first session. Things went well that night. The session was much more enjoyable than anything I experienced in the past. I even passed a urinalysis!

Back at home, I spoke with my wife for the first time in days. We didn't speak for a week and she had no idea what I had been doing. She assumed I had been drinking at home alone or out partying the whole time. She blamed me for not letting her know what I was up to the past week. It was my fault I didn't call her. Everything was my fault! She wasn't even relieved I went to another treatment center. It didn't matter at this point. She informed me of her intent to divorce me. She let me know the papers were being drafted. She didn't want to be with an active alcoholic and she didn't want to raise our daughter in that environment. I agreed with her on all accounts, except for the divorce. I was actively seeking treatment! I knew I'd never have a life, much less a marriage or relationship with my daughter if I kept drinking. Why couldn't she see that I was trying to get rid of my demon? Why couldn't she see how hard I was working? She couldn't answer any questions and it was obvious she had enough. I suppose I couldn't blame her, but I could still resent her.

She explained how she would come to Louisiana for the weekend and present the divorce papers to me in person. We could go over a few things and I could see my daughter while she was with me. She told me she was doing that as a favor to save me the embarrassment of a parish sheriff coming to my home. What a joke. I played along while still begging her to hold off. She kept telling me alcohol was the cause of all our problems. I was already sober though. I was already sober and she still had her mind made up to leave. I was dumbfounded. I knew it was just a week sober, but it was the beginning of something. I got rid of the only thing keeping me from being the greatest father and husband anyone could ever want. I got rid of the demon holding me down. I got rid of my enemy and I was learning how to live a life free from my addiction. Why was she still so adamant about leaving me?

I didn't sleep much that night or the next. I was lost during the day and stared at the ceiling fan all night. "Things aren't supposed to happen this way. Things are supposed to get better when you stop drinking. I'm supposed to hit my bottom, quit drinking, and everything gets better." I kept telling myself those things over and over again while sitting in the silence of the night.

The house was quiet Saturday morning. I sat there alone, without a single light or television turned on. I didn't want anything to disturb my thoughts. My family was away on a trip and the timing couldn't have been any better. I wouldn't have been able to handle everything with my wife if they were home. I was doing my best to prepare myself mentally and reality set. She drove up as I was drinking coffee in the kitchen. I couldn't move at first. I looked out the window to see her step out the car and begin unbuckling my daughter. The sight of that little angel broke me free from my frozen state.

My wife greeted me with a halfcocked smile as I opened the door. I could tell she was forcing it just to be nice. I may have done the same in return. I can't recall. My focus went to my daughter and I snatched her up as quickly as I could. All of the breath left my body as I hugged her firmly. It was a passionate hug. One that you would give someone you loved if it were the last time you would see them. She looked at me with her big blue eyes and I could tell they were filled with love. That look gave me enough strength to handle whatever her mother would throw at me that weekend.

Once my daughter turned her attention to playing around the house, we began to talk things over. We were both feeling each other out at this point. I didn't know if she was still sure about her decision to leave me. She was probably trying to figure out if I had been drinking. I was a week sober at this point with no intentions on ever having another drink. I must have displayed something sincere because she told me that she could sense a difference in me. She knew I was serious and she knew I was beginning to do better. I was already living a healthier, more productive life. Seeing this change must not have meant much though. She wanted to follow through with an appointment to sell the house I was living in when I called my parents for help. I agreed to comply and we got ready to meet the realtor that afternoon.

It was an uneventful ride to the house as we talked a little and acted as things were normal. I say it was normal. We didn't know what normal was anymore. We engaged each other in small talk. I could tell she was nervous about seeing the house. It would be the first time in months.

We masked our troubles as we pulled in the driveway. The realtor was already there, sitting in her car. I tried to stay away from them after instructing the realtor I'd help as much as possible. I walked around the yard and driveway. I played with my daughter as she walked around. Staying inside the place was not an option for me. The place haunted me still.

We left after the realtor. I had agreed to empty the home by the end of the next week and the meeting was done. We were walking out when something came up. A large dose of reality hit me in the jaw with a stone fist. I became flushed and couldn't speak. I drove my wife and daughter there, but couldn't do it anymore. I couldn't pretend. I could barely function. "I'm not driving back. You can get in the driver's seat of your car after buckling the little one in to her car seat. I'm done." I walked away to smoke a cigarette before leaving, trembling as I tried to take a drag. A few moments struggling with myself and I returned to the passenger seat of the car. We didn't speak a word to each other.

My wife pulled in to a coffee shop a few miles down the road and asked if I wanted anything as she stopped in the drive through. My stomach was twisted in knots and turned upside down. How could she eat or drink anything? How could she think I would be able to eat or drink anything? "No, I'm good. Thank you for asking." That's as nice as I could be to her. I was trying my best to respect the woman while trying to figure out how she could be so calm. She was struggling, too. She showed me by pulling in a parking spot after getting her ice coffee. She broke down crying right next to me and I had no idea how to react. "Why couldn't you sober up months ago? Why are you able to do this now? Why do you do this once I've decided to file for divorce? The papers are filed! My lawyer is paid!"

I stepped out of the car for a moment to gather my thoughts. "Where is she going with this?" There was no figuring it out so I opened the door once again and slid back in the seat. "I can't answer those questions. I can only tell you that I have been trying. I found a place where I fit in and I'm sober. I'm sober without any prescriptions, without any medication or anyone brainwashing me into thinking I need to be taking those things. I hope you decide to put a hold on going through with a divorce. You said yourself there is a noticeable difference in me already. It'll only get better from here. You have seen me at my worst. You have been with me through the hardest times. Please don't cut our relationship short by not giving us a chance. I want you to see me for who I really am. I want you to be by my side while I'm sober. I know we can have a beautiful future with our daughter." She cried uncontrollably as I spoke to her. I could tell she was pissed at me for everything that was done. She didn't deserve it and I knew that to be true. We eventually got back on the road without much more being said. She told me a few things she had been doing and the atmosphere in the car lightened a little.

With no real answer as to how she was feeling after everything was said in that parking lot, she pulled in to a local grocery store. She asked if I would cook dinner for them. I agreed and I started to believe things were looking good for us. "Why would she want me to cook for them and have a nice family meal if she still wants to leave?" I was excited to walk in the store and shop for groceries as a family. Activities like that were exactly what I had been missing. We got a few items and I was set to cook a nice Cajun meal that night.

Things weren't so serious as we got home to my parent's house and unloaded the groceries. I started cooking and put the radio on low. It was the classic country Saturday night on one of the local radio stations. I grew up on that stuff. Those oldies went together with rice and gravy better than anything! I thought I might even get a dance at some point.

Fifteen minutes in and my wife came to me with a notebook. She had already started figuring out how we would be dividing belongings, debt, and our time with our daughter. I choked up. My grip tightened on the spoon in my right hand as I stirred in the pot. I wanted her by my side so bad. I wanted her support so bad. I wanted to be a family more than anything in the world. "So this is what we will be talking about tonight?" I asked while clearing my throat. She replied swiftly. "Yes, we need to handle these things now. I filed in Texas so it'll be done in sixty days if we agree on the terms. You won't even need to hire a lawyer. I already paid the retainer on mine and he can handle the whole thing if we agree." I went along with what she was telling me to prevent confrontation. I had no energy to argue. "Time with my daughter is the only thing I'm concerned about. I'll keep my debt. You keep your debt. We each keep the things we had before we were married and we will split the rest. The house is your problem as you requested I back off and let you sell it." She agreed, wrote some notes, and the pad was put away. I continued cooking while staring blindly into the pot.

My daughter entered the kitchen, babbling and walking around through my legs. She was just what I needed to keep from breaking down over the stove. "Louisiana Woman, Mississippi Man" by Conway Twitty and Loretta Lynn started playing on the radio about that time and my fifteen-month-old daughter started dancing right in front of me. She had no idea what her mom and dad were going through. The pure love in her eyes looking at us showed a perfect example of the innocence in front of me. I slowly grew an uncontrollable smile and stopped what I was doing to dance with her. That radio station rolled straight in to "Coal Miner's Daughter" by Loretta Lynn and whisked my little one up into my arms. We danced around the kitchen while I tried to hide my tears from my wife. I didn't want her to see how much I was hurt.

We ate a while later as few words were spoken. My wife complimented the meal and I politely accepted. I cleaned the kitchen as she got our daughter ready for bed. I went outside so smoke a cigarette before getting cleaned up. I needed the time alone.

Awkward times continued that night. I walked in my bedroom to find my wife and daughter laying there, watching television. My wife was even on "my side" of the bed. I didn't have the heart so say anything. I thought about leaving the room for an empty bed down the hall, but I wanted to be next to my daughter. I didn't know when I'd see her again as my wife was talking about only allowing me one weekend a month with supervised visitation. So, I slid under the covers and held on the edge of the bed they occupied. I'd occasionally feel a foot softly pass mine and I'd move, hoping she would get the hint. "Why would she want to touch me?" I was not having physical contact that night. My daughter fell asleep quickly and I wasn't far behind her. My difference was sleep lasted for only an hour for me. I'd wake up to look over at the two sleeping soundly next to me and that view remained until morning. I tried to fall back asleep. My mind wasn't having it.

Sunday was another dreaded day, but with a twist. I'll get to that in a little while. Okay, so we woke up and played with our daughter for a while. We acted as though we were a family. We made our way to the kitchen for coffee and breakfast. I cut a banana for my daughter and poured her a cup of milk. She enjoyed that while I made myself some oatmeal for us to share. Sounds like a normal Sunday, just like any other a family may experience. My wife presented her W-2 to me so I could go ahead and finish our taxes. It needed to be done and I figured it was best to go ahead and get them done. That took me an hour or so and I received a phone call from my grandmother just as I was entering our direct deposit information for the refund. She invited us to have lunch with her and my grandfather. Other family members, cousins, were going to their house as well. I agreed we would visit with them since I had my daughter and I didn't know when or if they would get another chance to see her. I told my wife about it and she was good with the plans. What I didn't know was that she decided to present me with the divorce papers to sign right after I finished our tax returns and just before we were going to leave for my grandparents' house.

I started shaking and tears rolled from my face as I signed those papers. My signature wasn't very legible and the paper was stained with my tears, but it served her purpose. She quietly collected the documents while assuring me I only signed an acknowledgement of notice. Simply put, I signed a paper saying I was aware she wanted a divorce. I didn't care. I couldn't read the words through the heavy tears. Luckily, I had a twenty-minute drive to collect myself before facing my family. They had no idea all of this was going on at the moment.

We agreed to keep things between the two of us and we did just that. The acting hats went on before exiting the car and we pretended everything was good. Lunch was delicious and we had a good visit with my family. We left after a couple of hours as my wife and daughter had to drive back to Texas.

Back at my parent's house, I helped my wife load the car while my daughter was playing. That's about the time when my wife turned to me with a concerned look in her eyes. She explained her living situation was undesirable as she was in the process of moving in a new apartment. Her cousin was evicted from the home they were living in due to complications in her own divorce. I listened as she explained she would be moving things for most the week and she didn't even have a bed in the place. "Can our daughter stay with you this week?" She was emotional as she asked this of me. She hadn't been away from our daughter for a week straight, ever. I calmly agreed as I was doing her a favor, struggling to hide my excitement. It was so unexpected and I was so happy to spend the next seven days with her. I longed for time with my daughter.

We said our goodbyes as she got in her car. She hugged and kissed our little one. I pleaded my case to her once again, begging her to hold off on the divorce. I kissed her as she reluctantly sat there. She told me that she thought it was best for her to be on her own. We each needed to work on our own issues. I needed to prove to her I stopped drinking because she felt like she couldn't trust anything I said or did. I asked her to think things over and the conversation was done. She closed her door and left for Texas. I stood there with my daughter in my arms, watching her go when it hit me. "She just said she doesn't trust me. She just bluntly told me that I need to prove myself to her because she was skeptical about whether or not I quit drinking." I looked at my daughter in my arms, realized my wife just left her with me for a week, and her excuse for leaving me was that she didn't trust I was sober. "What the fuck was this woman thinking?!?!"

Truth is, I had quit drinking over a week before their visit and was confident in my abilities to continue healing. As if I didn't have enough motivation before, the little girl in my arms multiplied my desire for success more than words would explain. My wife didn't know any of these things, though. She blindly contradicted every reason for her desire to divorce me while driving away without our daughter. I was strangely comfortable.

High Road to Recovery

I was on cloud nine when she left. I stopped dwelling on my wife leaving me and concentrated on the beautiful little girl in my presence. We played and spent time together. I didn't know how things would go, but I knew it was going to be good. My parents got back home later that evening and were both excited to see my daughter. We enjoyed our time together catching up and talking about how the week was going to go. I didn't have work for another week and a half so I told them I planned to stay home with her during the day and they could watch her in the evenings for me when I had counseling scheduled. The only thing I had scheduled was to get my truck to the shop to be fixed from my recent blunder. I had an appointment on the Thursday morning so we planned for a sitter so I could drive there and back. It would just be a half day trip since I planned to leave during early morning hours while everyone slept.

Okay, so Monday came around and we had a great day. I had a new book to read so I did that while my daughter played and watched cartoons. I was enjoying her company so much. Also my mom insisted we go shopping for my daughter that evening since my wife didn't leave any clothes that fit her. We understood she hadn't originally planned to leave my little girl behind, but we had absolutely nothing for her.

We went to the mall that night and spent some quality time together while getting my little one some clothes and shoes. I was fortunate enough for my dad to get her some diapers, wipes, and other stuff like that earlier during the day.

Tuesday and Wednesday were more good days. I would spend the day with my daughter and go to counselling in the evening. She fell asleep before I got home the first night, but she stayed up to go to bed with me the second night. I was so happy to see her greet me at the door.

I left at three o'clock in the morning that Thursday and headed west for Texas. The drive was smooth and easy. Traffic was light and flowed seamlessly as I had my cruise control set just above seventy miles per hour. I stopped a few miles away from the shop for a coffee and a bathroom break. As I returned to my truck, I checked the time and decided to continue to the shop. I would be a few minutes early, but I figured it would give me time to go over everything with the guys that would be working on the truck. I had an appointment for a rental car company to pick me up from the shop at eight thirty that morning, giving me a little over an hour for discussions and a break from driving.

I got to that shop and talked things over with the guys, but it all happened faster than I anticipated. We finished all the details well before eight o'clock and now I suddenly had some time to kill. The crew was nice and they visited with me for a little bit, but I mostly talked with the manager in the office. There was a beautiful young lady that worked in the shop office as well. I spoke with her from time to time over the past months while ordering parts, but I felt awkward seeing her in person. I was attracted to her and I could tell there was something about the way she looked at me. The timing made it weird for me. I didn't know what to think about my marital status. I know what you're thinking; I did some shitty stuff months before. There's a big difference this time around though. Did you guess it? I'm sober!

Well the rental company let me down as they didn't show up at their appointment time. I called and they told me they were trying to catch up, but someone should be over to pick me up within an hour. I ended the phone call and sat back down at the end of their counter. She overheard my conversation and picked on me a little. It was friendly and just enough to "break the ice". We visited as she prepared orders. We talked about my truck, past trucks, her vehicle, past vehicles, likes, dislikes, stuff like that. After a while, relationship type questions started coming about. I mentioned overhearing she was in a relationship. She asked about my marriage. Through our awkwardness, we clicked. We flirted with each other while talking about how we didn't remember how to flirt. We talked about how it had been longer than we could remember since we asked someone out or tried starting up a new relationship. After a few hours of visiting with her, she left for lunch and my rental car showed up. It all happened by chance and I left with a warm feeling. My truck was in the back of my mind as I started driving to Louisiana, that beautiful lady was involved in all of my thoughts.

I called my family while travelling east through Texas. I let them know that I was running late due to the rental company holding me up. I got an update on my daughter and everything was good. I had enough gas to get close to home so I wasn't stopping anytime soon. "East bound with the hammer down."

I made it within about forty miles of my parent's house when I had to stop for gas. It had been a long day, but a positive day. I took my time, used the restroom, grabbed a soft drink, and pumped some gas. Everything was nice and upbeat. I had just started my rental when my phone rang with a number I did not recognize. "Hello. Yes, this is he. I see. Well it was good while it lasted. Could you please let me know a final date to close out my ticket? We can set up a date and time to meet directly after the final date given by the client. No, no thank you." I put the car in "Drive" and pulled over by the curb before returning the shifter to the "Park" position. I slumped over in my seat with my head pressed against the window and stayed in that position for a while. The car was running and the radio was off. The air conditioner gave a gentle background noise as I listened in a state of confusion. Five days after receiving divorce papers from my wife, eleven days sober, the day I dropped my truck off at a shop to have extensive work done, I was laid off from my consulting position offshore. My offshore career would never be the same. My life would never be the same. I eventually drove away from that parking lot and drove the rest of the way home in silence. I didn't say a word about what had occurred in that call; except for a text message to my wife. When I got back to my parent's house, I sent her a courtesy text. She had been after me to pay daycare and the mortgage on the house. I was done with the house as soon as I signed it off to her, but I wanted to help with things involving my daughter. I let her know I was unemployed as of that afternoon and wouldn't be able to help.

We had a quiet night at home. I played with my daughter and went to bed early with her. We watched cartoons and tried to rest. My anxiety wore me down that afternoon. She would lie next to me and put her little head on my chest. It was the greatest feeling in the world and I felt as though I needed her more than she needed me.

We had a great couple days together after that. I bottled up my emotions about the layoff, refusing to let it affect my time with my daughter. I could break down the following week. It wasn't going to get me down now.

We went to church Sunday morning and I savored my last minutes with her. Two weeks sober, even with a divorce and layoff. I felt like I was doing the deal as spent that week with my daughter. I thought about our times together and wondered when I'd see her again. Time passed quickly that day as I headed to our meeting point. We spoke briefly and my daughter was gone before I knew it. This would prove to be the first of many awkward meetings to exchange custody of my daughter.

Back home that evening, I started mentally preparing for my upcoming week. It would be a couple of weeks before I'd see my daughter again, but I'd need to concentrate on my recovery anyways. I continued to read in my books and attended my counselling session without fail. I even got family to come with me to the house when I finished removing belongings. It was a place that triggered me. The place haunted me. I felt the presence of evil when I entered the driveway and I could never shake that feeling. If that wasn't enough, my dad and I pulled up for the very last time and got one last surprise. I opened the back door and stepped in the house to find a Raven sitting on the couch in the living room. Yes, a large black bird was in the home, waiting for me. I was petrified at first. And we got the message. I opened the doors and some windows hoping it would leave. We grabbed the last few items I had in the place while that bird sat, staring at us. Just as we finished, I heard a noise that got my attention. I turned to see the Raven walking on the living room floor. It slowly made its way toward me as I was standing outside. We were suspiciously looking at each other as if we were waiting on the other's next move. Once the bird made it to the threshold of the back door, it suddenly flew away. That was it. We closed up the place and I left the property for the last time, leaving another chapter of my life behind.

The next couple of weeks went without a hitch. I was making every counseling session and even enjoying it. My counselor showed genuine concern towards my recovery. She even periodically asked me about how my divorce was going. She helped me with setting boundaries to ensure I didn't let my wife drive me back to drinking. I say it that way, but don't misunderstand. I knew enough to know it wouldn't be anyone else's fault if I drank again. It would prove to be solely my fault if I were to let anyone get to me. I was looking within to fix these things.

The time came for me to pick my daughter up from her mother once again. I was still clinging to some hope of us reconciling and would try to speak with her periodically. She wasn't having it. She told me it was absolutely what she wanted and maybe we could get back together a couple of years down the road. I had no idea what she was thinking by telling me that, but something came over me where I was realizing my marriage was, in fact, done. The exchange was brief. We barely spoke. My nerves were shot as I was so anxious in the days leading up to getting my daughter. We didn't have any orders. I didn't even have an attorney. So I was skeptical as I knew she could have backed out and kept my daughter from me. My worries were settled as I saw her car sitting in the parking lot of our meeting spot.

I had a fantastic weekend with my daughter, though it passed by quickly. We had our quality time and were back in the car headed to her mother before I knew it. The exchange was quick and I left in tears. I was isolated from my family. Well, I was isolated from the two people I chose to be my family. Reality began setting in as I was now a month sober and able to think about other parts of my life besides recovery.

I began looking for an attorney that following week. I called multiple local family law practices only to find out I had to retain counsel from the country my wife filed petition. Shit! "How am I supposed to find a good attorney that'll treat me right in a place where I don't know anyone?" I looked over plenty of law firms over that week and one stood out to me. I found a family law attorney in a family practice that gave me the "warm and fuzzy" feeling. She closely resembled my soon to be ex-wife and even went to the same school. To make things better, she was a Father's Rights advocate. I set up a phone interview for her next availability.

My body was tense as I picked up the phone to call in to that attorney. They put me on a brief hold and then a calming voice was heard on the line. The lady speaking to me was the lead attorney. Her knowledge showed through immediately and it didn't take long before I sensed she was genuine. We were soon talking like best friends and I knew I could trust her. I took notes during our two-hour phone call and I felt good as I hung up the phone. "These are the people I need to protect me." I thought about everything as I sighed in relief. I sent in a deposit a couple of days later. "Let the legal games begin!"

The wife found out about my attorney when she received our contested petition. She made me feel very uncomfortable about things coming up with my daughter and splitting things up. We contested as my attorney found some things in the original petition disturbing as well.

These actions didn't help things between my wife and me. We were scared to talk with each other about anything, really. I was defensive and constantly watching over my shoulder. We resorted to talking only about matters specific to the wellbeing of our daughter. Things got worse for me around this time as well. My health insurance dropped me due to my recent layoff. I was about a month in to my counselling and five weeks sober when I received the phone call. "Sir, I am calling from the recovery center you attend outpatient counseling. We were informed you no longer have health insurance as of yesterday. I have a price quote for you if you wish to continue attending our counseling in the evenings." "Ma'am, I have a session tonight. I was already preparing to leave to go over there." "Sir, you can come, but you will be charged for the session. As it is, you owe for the one you attended last night." Well, that ended my counselling at the place. I was upset, but determined to continue on my path to recovery. I had a beautiful little girl that needed her father.

I started going to more AA meetings to supplement my recovery with this sudden abundance of free time. Also, it was time to pick up my truck from the shop in Houston! I pulled a trailer there to pick it up and was at the shop before seven o'clock in the morning. I beat half of the people that worked there! So excited to have it back and see everything that was done, I was overwhelmed with joy. I drove right up to the parking lot and hopped out to walk to my crew cab. It was beautiful. I started talking to some of the guys about it and they started putting parts in the other truck I drove there with the trailer. That pretty lady got to work about this time. We spotted each other as she stepped out her car. I couldn't miss that beautiful smile and her eyes captivated me. Her big brown eyes glistened gold against her olive skin. She completely distracted me from the reason I was there. Shit, I forgot what I was doing at the moment I saw her. All I could manage to do was say, "Good morning."

The shop owner came over to me and there was something he didn't like about the way my truck was washed, so he had the guys come over and wash it again. That was fine with me. I grabbed my coffee from the other truck and walked over to the office. We visited some more that morning. I was in a different state of mind as I spoke with her that morning. I was attracted to her. She was in the best mood and a pleasure to share conversation. I could tell she got dressed quick because she was wearing a tee shirt and jeans with her hair a mess. It was the cutest thing I saw in months. Almost an hour after I walked in the office to speak with her, one of the guys came in to let me know my truck was ready to load up. I smiled at her and she reminded me to take a copy of my receipt before leaving. She handed my paperwork to me and in one last effort to flirt with her, I made a quick statement. "You have my cell number on your copy of the invoice. Give me a call anytime and we can do something when I come back to Houston. And remember you have a friend in Louisiana if you want to get away for a weekend."

People were taking pictures of my beautiful truck riding the trailer as I drove down the interstate. I was thoroughly enjoying my morning headed home. Half way back to Louisiana, I got a random text message. "How's your drive going? Everything okay?" I waited a few minutes to reply as I was planning to stop for gas at the next station. I didn't recognize the number, but I had a good feeling I knew who was sending me the message. I could picture her sitting behind the counter in the shop office and typing her message. I replied with the standard "Hey, who is this? And yes, my drive is going well. Getting lots of attention while pulling this beautiful truck down the road." She replied, letting me know it was her and mentioned she wasn't sure if she should be talking to me. I don't know if she ever truly explained what made her feel that way, but the hesitation was put aside. We talked on the phone an hour or so later while she took her lunch break. We continued to talk on the phone that evening and every day following.

Back at home that afternoon, I was excited. I unloaded the truck and took a little drive around town with it. There seemed to be a couple of bugs I needed to work out, but I was happy. I took notes while riding around and planned to get in to fixing some of the problems myself. My new lady called me again that evening and we talked for a while. She was just getting out of a similar relationship and we confided in each other as we got deeper in conversations.

The next day, I was determined to get my truck set up. I went ride again to put a few miles on it and try to pinpoint a couple of electrical issues. Something came over me while I was out. I had to stop at the store for gas and experienced another issue with the truck. The fuel filler wouldn't accept gas. I had to go back in the store for my refund and without thinking gave instruction for a pint of rum. I got back in my truck and poured the rum in to two soft drinks I bought along with it. The bottle was thrown in the trash at the pump before I proceeded to drive home from the station. I'm not sure why, but I didn't drink any of it right away and that was fortunate. The truck made an awkward noise as I travelled down a two-lane road with the cruise set at a modest pace. It was enough to get my attention. I jumped up in my seat and listened closely to figure out if it was still making any odd noises. I didn't need to be that alert. My floor jumped as I heard the next loud noise. The truck slowed with the noise and I continued to hear something beating on the bottom of the truck. It came to a stop in the middle of the road. A car pulled up behind my truck a few seconds later and a gentleman offered to help me push it to a side street. I was lucky to get off of the road. A friend of mine answered my call as I stood next to the truck. He didn't live far away and wasn't busy. I lucked out once again. He picked me up, gave me a ride back home to get the other truck and trailer, then followed me back to help me load up. Again, I don't know what crossed my mind to ask for a bottle that day. I was happy to ruin my sobriety after the truck broke, though. All I wanted after the breakdown was to have a drink. Nothing else mattered as I reached for the one of the two drinks in my truck. I didn't give myself a chance to break the obsession. They were in my reach.

I went to bed that night with mixed feelings. I relapsed after at least six weeks of sobriety, but it was kept to just the two drinks. My mind seemed to easily justify the actions. No negative consequences were experienced in this time and no one knew. I didn't tell anyone any better either. The next day seemed to drag as I struggled with my decision to drink the day before. Those thoughts ended as I looked over to my truck and trailer loaded up and parked next to the driveway. I made a couple of phone calls to let the shop know I needed to take it back to them. They spoke with me for a while and ensured me they would leave a spot open for me the next day. Plans were set and I was ready to prepare for my travel day. My new friend and I spoke on the phone that evening and made plans for the next evening. She was excited to see me and I was eager to have a date. The divorce and personal struggles in my life kept me from having any kind of social life.

The alarm went off at three o'clock the next morning. I barely slept while lying in bed that night. My mind was racing as I wondered about how the drive would go. I wondered about how our date would go, too. The affects I experienced that night were similar to what I would do to myself every night before leaving for work offshore. Anxiety would take over as my body tried to rest. So, my excitement for the next day allowed me to hop out of bed. My bag was already packed and ready to go. A cup of coffee with a hot shower did the trick to finish waking me up. I drank a second cup of coffee while my truck warmed up, then it was time to get going. The caffeine in my body would be plenty to keep my going until the truck ran out of gas. I didn't have to stop until I was in Texas and almost to the shop.

The guys were waiting for me when I pulled up. The pretty girl in the office was waiting, also. She had a better idea of when I was going to get there, though. We talked during the second half of my trip. Regardless, the guys were ready and I was able to back up directly to the lift they opened for my truck. They unloaded and told me not to worry about leaving. They wanted to assess the damage and possibly repair it right away. I didn't mind it as we hung out in the office. We got caught up in visiting, talking about all sorts of things as the mechanic walked in to let me know the truck was fixed. They had already gone through it to find the electrical problems and sent another mechanic to the driveline shop for my driveshaft issues. I went for a ride with the mechanic as he explained everything to me, then he loaded me up. I could have gone back home that same day, but I wasn't missing my date. It was a quick ride to the hotel, not quick enough. I spotted a liquor shop before getting to my hotel and couldn't let myself pass it up. I grabbed a pack of soft drinks and bottle of my favorite 100 proof rum. I didn't want to get drunk that night, just have a drink or two while sitting at the hotel to help settle my nerves. I still bought a fifth of the stuff, convinced I'd save the rest for after my trip.

I accomplished all of this and settled in to my room by around two that afternoon. My friend was coming to meet me around six or seven that evening. I used my down time to walk around the hotel area and grab a burger with fries. It was fun relaxing a little while checking out the place. I eventually made my way back to my room to work on that bottle a while. I didn't really enjoy it as I was so worried about sticking to my plan. I refused to ruin my night and my date's night. The first drink went down easy regardless of my anxiety. I put the bottle away as I prepared my second drink. A second one could be handled, but a third would get me in trouble.

She got to my hotel just as she planned. I was anxiously waiting for her. Neither of us had been out on a first date like this in years! It was so new to us, but we were able to embrace the nerves and uncertainties. We began joking about it where we were able connect on a deeper level. I knew she was in to me when she got out of her car at the hotel after dinner. She wanted to get down and I was excited to spend more time together. That's just what we did. We kicked back in bed and watched shitty late night television while getting to know each other better. She stayed for much of the night as we found something special in one another. We weren't sure what it was, but it was good.

She did, in fact, do something special for me. I went back to bed after walking her out and completely forgot about that bottle. I went back to bed and slept soundly. I woke up to messages from her on my phone, immediately putting a smile on my face. I took my time in getting dressed and eventually packed my truck up to leave. My procrastination was somewhat due to my hopes of possibly having lunch together, but I knew it wasn't going to happen. She wasn't ever able to get away for a solid lunch break. Things were great though.

The drive went without a hitch. I took my time pulling the trailer back and things were going well. What I'd like to highlight here is the beginning of a deathly habit. A few hours in to my drive, I had to pull over for some gas. The station I picked was nice because it was easily accessible and it marked about an hour of driving left to get home. I found something else at that station. They had a wonderful liquor store! I didn't miss the opportunity to grab a bottle of my favorite 100 proof rum while I was in there. The bottle of left over rum from my hotel stay wasn't enough for me. It was insignificant as my mind told me that I needed a full bottle. I still couldn't explain the obsession, except I opened a door that had been closed for the previous six weeks. Back on the road, I didn't drink and drive. I wasn't going to risk that, well I wasn't going to risk it far from the house. My next stop was about a ten to fifteen minute drive from home and I sure did make a drink and indulged just prior to turning in my driveway. It was the only one I would have until bedtime that night. I unloaded the truck from the trailer and parked everything out of my family's way. I unpacked bags and settled back in the house. It had been a long day and I had a slight buzz from that drink, so it was time to kick back and continue drinking while watching television. Interesting thing, I didn't even bother with the bottle that was already open. I drank the entire bottle I bought that day, as if I were saving the other one for backup or something.

Well the next day proved to show why that backup alcohol was lurking. I was still drunk when I woke up that morning. The first thought crossing my mind was about my day. I didn't have any plans to leave the house. My second thought, well that was more of an action. I reached for the bottle and flipped it upside down to my lips. "Nothing like straight 100 proof rum to the pallet while you're still lying in bed!" I had several large gulps of the drink, turned the television on and eventually passed out again. A couple more hours of sleep and I woke up feeling good, meaning I was still drunk. I decided to mess around at home and wash my truck. I'd make plans for the next day as I needed to run a few errands. I don't remember much else as I continued drinking throughout the day, but I do know I was back in bed early that evening.

The next day was interesting to say the least. I woke up early and felt like shit as I left the house. My head was throbbing, mouth dry, eyes seemed to jump around, and my body tingled as I fought cold sweats. I made it twenty minutes in to my drive when I stopped for a pint of vodka to mix with some juice. My first planned stop was going to take a couple of hours so I felt comfortable having a drink as I pulled up to the place. "Surely it will wear off to an acceptable level by the time I'll be leaving. I got this. It'll make me feel better so I can get through today." My demon was in full force and I was in submission.

I finished at that place and completed the rest of my errands. I got a late lunch on the way home and enjoyed a crisp, cold beer with my sandwich. My next stop was a store located about ten minutes away from my family's home and it was all about getting another bottle. I'd pick up vodka this time and stash it away in my truck for when I got home. The voice in my head was telling me I would need vodka over anything else so no one would smell it on my breath.

Dreams of a Drunk

I slept with very vivid dreams that night. Memories of bumping another car felt so vivid, they frightened me. I'm no stranger to vivid dreams. Ones that felt more real than reality itself. That experience didn't help curb my feelings though. I had flashes of being in traffic and bumping a car that slammed the breaks in front of me. In my dream, I ran

from the event as the impact was very minor. I had flashes
of driving fast, but not much over the speed limit. I didn't
want to draw extra attention to myself. These thoughts ran
back and forth through my mind all night. I was drunk from
my evening drinks in bed, but they felt so real. The clock
seemed to click with a slow rhythm as I patiently waited for
my family to leave for work. I didn't want them to see me
checking for damage on my truck. I needed to see there
was nothing wrong!

Sure enough, everyone was out of the house by about seven that morning. I always stayed to myself in my room with the door closed and it was understood I slept in until eight or nine. I was usually awake and hiding from everyone, though. I didn't want questions. I didn't have the energy to be around my family. Isolation was always easier for me. Anyways, I made my way outside to my truck to find no damage on it. I stood there looking at it for thirty minutes or so. The memories from the night were false. I even buffed the front of the truck to find the smallest blemish, but couldn't find a thing!

Another week of drinking everything I could find at home, I found myself taking part in a quiet ride with my dad. My parents wanted to help, but didn't know what to do besides pay for me to complete my outpatient program. My dad and I went for that drive without saying more than a word to each other. I didn't know where we were headed when we left the house, but I figured it had something to do with treatment. "Is this the road I turn left on?" He asked as we neared the street where I had attended treatment earlier this year. I answered with a quick "Yes" as I knew exactly where we were headed.

Once inside the place, my dad asked for someone we could speak with about payment options. He turned to me and explained his offer. He explained how it could be possible for me to attend outpatient treatment, but they couldn't afford to provide me with any more intensive treatment. I was okay with that, but my motives at this point were not so genuine anymore. See, I had already figured out how to get away with drinking during treatment and now I could continue providing clean drug and alcohol test reports to my divorce attorney. I could accomplish that while still doing what I wanted to do. So, we visited with a lady in the office and I was set to begin treatment the following week.

Enough is Enough

The same week I was returning to treatment presented another surprise. My wife started talking to me like she wanted to reconcile. I was confused and emotional, but jumped at the opportunity to discuss things in person. I don't believe I ever communicated my feelings to her effectively, though I wanted nothing more than to live a "happy ever after" kind of life with her and my daughter. So with my bags quickly packed, I was driving to her home. We talked things through and with everything we could have concentrated on, my mind was hung up on her love life since I had been absent. We shouldn't have even let ourselves go there in questioning each other. Problem is, I've always been obsessed with "not being that guy". I was petrified of looking like a fool in front of others if we got back together and they knew she slept around in the meantime. It blinded me from the fact that I acted like a fool the whole time. The question finally came up during dinner. "Who have you been with since we split up?" I believe she was just as honest as I was while confessing my short-lived relationship. Our confessions had one significant difference though. She was still seeing they guy she had been with since we separated. I couldn't handle it.

I tried, but couldn't stop my mind from imagining her having sexual relations with another man. We spent an emotional night together as we both seemed in a weak state. Conversation turned physical the next morning as a hug led to a kiss. One kiss led to another. Our clothes were off and we were in her bed before either of us were to realize just how it would affect our future. Awkwardness and insecurities led to us both exiting her place quietly just ten minutes after making love for the last time.

I left Houston in a state of confusion. I was strangely optimistic of rekindling a relationship with my wife while struggling with knowing that can't be my reality. Before I left her, I said "I know I can't handle getting back together and it won't work, but I'm willing to try anyways." I ran those words through my head over and over while trying to think what kind of person I am to even say that to her. I thought about the last time I drank. "It was a few days ago. My brain is functioning correctly." I'd tell myself I meant those words and I couldn't even comprehend what I meant by it. Sunshine turned to rain about this point in the drive and my thoughts turned from possibilities of this relationship to concentrating on the drive. I quickly checked my mirror to see how my daughter was doing and she was sleeping. An angel in my backseat was snuggled up comfortably in her car seat, sleeping. My eyes watered as I stared down the rain soaked road ahead of me. How could this little person be so comfortable with me driving her? How could she sleep while I drive through this horrible weather? I felt overwhelmed.

I drove through to my usual exit where I liked to stop and put gas when returning from the Ex's apartment. This particular stop was special to me. It signaled I was less than an hour away from home and there was a security guard that worked the door. I'd wait until a spot right up front would open and park there with my truck running when my daughter was with me. I covered all the bases! I thought it out! My truck would be running with the air conditioner set on 70 degrees to keep her cool. I'd park right up front and give a little look to the guard as to let him know I needed him to watch my truck. My windows were tinted limousine dark so no one would even know if anyone was in the vehicle. The truck would be parked with her in it for less than five minutes. Most importantly, it usually took me two minutes to grab my bottle of 100 proof spiced rum and get back in my vehicle. I didn't have to worry about the interlock device timing out if it randomly started the standard six-minute count down. I didn't have to worry about anything happening to my daughter. I really had it figured out.

The stop I made on this day was like any other routine stop. I carried out the usual run in the store. My daughter had snacks so she was perfectly content. I grabbed a bottle and paid for it without waiting in line. It was routine. I even reminded myself it was only to settle my nerves if things got unbearable later that evening. I stowed the bottle conspicuously located in my clothes bag, pumped gas, and we were back on the road. My anxiety returned with the sunshine. How could she dare speak to me about getting back together while she was "casually" sleeping with someone? I understood why I was in the predicament. The whole reason was neatly tucked away in my travel bag, my coping mechanism. Fully understanding things felt like a curse. I had all the knowledge and understanding necessary to quit drinking and straighten everything out in my life. I was drowning in Self Will! What is even worse? I knew it.

My arrival to the house was just as I expected. My dad heard me drive up and immediately came see me at my truck. The constant bombardment annoyed every fiber of my being. I knew he loved my daughter and me so much that it was all in the best intentions, but I felt so smothered. He immediately started asking questions. "Can I help you carry something?" "Can I carry her for you?" my replies had to come off short as I was annoyed before he ever said a word. "No!" "She wants me to hold her and I can carry my bags!" Of course I didn't want him to help with a bag. He could magically feel the bottle I have stashed! Oh, the anxiety. The self-inflicted paranoia actually impressed me.

We moved our conversation in the house as I began putting my things away in my room. Questions moved towards the topic of my conversations with Ex. I was expecting this and dreading this, too. I didn't know what to tell myself. I couldn't tell anyone else about it. My answers were vaguely honest and short. He was satisfied and proceeded to tell me what I already knew was coming. "Your mother is going to want to know everything when she gets home in a couple hours so be patient with her and answer her." Wow, that's all I needed to hear to convince myself it was almost time for a drink.

I timed everything out as usual. I knew my daughter was going to stay with my mom all evening so I hit the bottle when I knew she was about thirty minutes away. That 100 proof rum had a little burn the first couple of swigs then all was numb. I drank a little to take the edge off before my mom got home and we then visited. I must have done myself good though. I know I didn't get drunk until after she was home, but I only remember us having a conversation. I don't remember the content at all. I remember walking outside with my daughter playing and we sat on a swing. I remember being back in the house and interrupting the conversation with a video call involving my Ex. Did I call her? Did she call me? I only know I went in my room to have privacy with the conversation. It went horribly. Anyone but her could have guessed that though. Well I couldn't have guessed it either. I had the conversation with her! What did we talk about? I know it involved her intentions with the man she was currently seeing and I focused on dwelling on that instead of our relationship. I don't know any other details.

Now I am off of the phone and listening to my family play with my daughter. I am an anxious, paranoid, mess feeling like I lost everything. I did lose everything! All I would have is time with my daughter and I can't even stay sober while dealing with life. She always asks for me. She always wants her daddy. I can want her internally, but know I can't have a relationship with her just as I can't have a relationship with anyone else in life. Alcohol has taken that from me. I curse the bottle while picking it up to take another sip. Now that you can imagine my state of mind, picture me walking out the bedroom and going to try and coax my daughter in to coming to play with me. I did these things while thinking she would make everything better. A verbal argument with my mother sent me walking back to my bedroom and dwelling on everything. I was miserable. I was done and under the influence of a demon that held me mercilessly for twenty years.

Something was different about this night. I do not remember any details about the conversations with others that evening. That was the usual blackout accompanying my liquor consumption. Later events of the night are quite vivid though.

I went to the closet and grabbed my 12-gauge shot gun my dad bought me when I was a kid. It was both a matter of convenience as the gun was close by and it was exactly the firearm I wanted for this shot. I was furious and felt trapped by the only two people who still loved me. These thoughts were racing through my mind as I searched for the high brass 4 shot shells. I reached in and grabbed one shell. That is all I would need. After inspecting the gun and shell, I loaded it with a swift stroke of the pump action and confirmed the gun chambered. The safety was set to fire and I set the gun next to my bed. Now it was time to wait. I wanted to hear my family go to sleep. I wanted to hear my daughter finish playing across the house and go silent.

Time seemed to crawl by as I sat back in bed watching the ceiling fan spin around. I wondered what would happen after I was gone. I thought about the initial pain some of my family would experience. I also thought of peace my parents would have in the long term. They wouldn't have to worry anymore! I would no longer be a burden to them. Then my daughter's playful scream would echo through the house and these thoughts would subside for a moment. My Ex wouldn't have to continue with a divorce case. She could call herself a widow and that's not bad at all. It puts everything on me. "Damn these dreaded thoughts are back."

The house eventually went silent and I still sat in the same position staring at the ceiling fan. My anger and emotions were still peaked. At this point in time, I began thinking of what the room would look like after the shot. "It'll be a mess!" Would they ever be able to go in it again? Oh well, benefits outweigh consequences. I swung my feet over the side of the bed and grabbed my trusty old shotgun for secondary inspection. All was good. The wood was smooth and felt right in my hands. The action of the pump and fire switch were still smooth and felt right. The steel smelled so good as I held the gun close to me.

Sitting on the edge of my bed, I set the butt of the gun on the floor and angled the shotgun where the barrel placed firmly on my sternum. My eyes closed, I prayed and asked for forgiveness. I couldn't seem to complete a prayer. I found myself becoming more frustrated. "I won't give anyone the satisfaction of even having an open casket." I whispered to myself as I removed the barrel from my chest and placed it under my jaw. "I'm not going to be one of the cries for help. No letter, just action for me. They can all wonder about my breaking point." As I stopped talking to myself, I found myself praying once again. My thoughts would take me through the whole scenario before I could finish a prayer. Finally fed up with trying to pray with God and let him know my sorrows, I had something to say. "YOU kept me alive and out of jail though I did so much wrong while drinking. YOU gave me a beautiful daughter and let me marry her mother, only for her to leave me months ago. YOU saved me from so much. Why? I'm about to ask in person before YOU deny my entry to Heaven. I can't believe it's come to this." With my chin still resting on the barrel of my favorite gun, I reached for the trigger with my bare foot and slipped the second toe of my right foot on the trigger. I pulled that trigger with tears flowing from my body at 03:53am in the morning. "CLICK"

Made in the USA
San Bernardino, CA
28 April 2017